BUSINESS ENGLISH FOR BEGINNERS

A1

MIKE HOGAN

BRITTA LANDERMANN

SHAUNESSY ASHDOWN

ADDITIONAL MATERIAL

ANDREW FROST, BERLIN

ADVISERS

LAWRENCE DAVIES, NÜRNBERG

INA HIERONYMUS, HALLE

LIESELOTTE KELLERMANN, WACKERSDORF

KENT LYON, MÜNCHEN

Business English for Beginners A1
Kursbuch

Im Auftrag des Verlages erarbeitet von

Mike Hogan, Britta Landermann und Shaunessy Ashdown
mit Unterstützung von Andrew Frost (Textbeiträge und Redaktion)

Beratende Mitarbeit

Lawrence Davies, Nürnberg

Ina Hieronymus, Halle

Lieselotte Kellermann, Wackersdorf

Kent Lyon, München

Redaktion

John Stevens, Rani Kumar (Projektkoordination)

Redaktionelle Mitarbeit

Christine House, Zsuzsa Parádi (Wortliste)

Bildredaktion

Uta Hübner, Rani Kumar

Projektleitung

Murdo MacPhail

Umschlaggestaltung

hawemannundmosch, bureau für konzeption und gestaltung, Berlin

Layout und technische Umsetzung

finedesign, Berlin

Illustration

Christian Bartz, Berlin

Zum vorliegenden Kursbuch sind auch erhältlich:
Workbook ISBN 978-3-06-020661-2
Teaching Guide ISBN 978-3-06-020664-3

www.cornelsen.de

1. Auflage, 3. Druck 2014

Alle Drucke dieser Auflage sind inhaltlich unverändert und können im Unterricht nebeneinander verwendet werden.

Druck: Firmengruppe APPL, aprinta Druck, Wemding

ISBN 978-3-06-020658-2

PEFC zertifiziert

Dieses Produkt stammt aus nachhaltig bewirtschafteten Wäldern und kontrollierten Quellen

PEFC/04-32-0928   www.pefc.de

Welcome to Business English for Beginners

Mit dem neuen **Business English for Beginners A1** sind Sie auf dem sicheren Weg in die englische Sprache. Alles ist darauf ausgerichtet, dass Sie zeitsparend, praxisorientiert und effizient für Ihren beruflichen Alltag lernen.

Jede Unit bietet Ihnen ein klar strukturiertes Thema mit aktuellem Praxisbezug aus dem Geschäftsleben. Die Lernziele (➜ *Learning objectives*) am Anfang der *Unit* verdeutlichen, was auf den folgenden Seiten erreicht werden kann. Die insgesamt sieben *Units* bestehen jeweils aus vier Abschnitten.

Die *Introduction* bietet Ihnen einen leichten Einstieg in das neue Thema. Im Abschnitt *Business and Office Skills* werden die Grundlagen für die neuen Strukturen und Sprachmittel gelegt und durch zahlreiche Übungen gefestigt. Sie lernen so schnell und sicher auf Englisch E-Mails zu schreiben, zu telefonieren oder in Meetings zu kommunizieren. Auf der *Grammar*-Seite finden Sie übersichtliche Grammatikzusammenfassungen und verständliche Erläuterungen mit Querverweisen auf zusätzliche Übungen. Die *Units* werden durch den Abschnitt *Consolidation* abgerundet. Hier werden die Inhalte der gesamten *Unit* noch einmal in Übungen miteinander verwoben und gemeinsam im Unterricht vertieft.
Für das Selbststudium ist außerdem ein **Workbook** erhältlich, mit dem das Erlernte weiter gefestigt und vertieft werden kann.

Ein besonderer Pluspunkt von **Business English for Beginners A1** sind die vielen Hörverständnisübungen auf der mitgelieferten Audio-CD. Wie in der internationalen Geschäftswelt, begegnen Sie hier englischsprachigen Menschen aus der ganzen Welt. Damit Sie das Gelernte sofort anwenden können, sind die Hörtexte mit einem Augenmerk auf natürliche Sprache gewählt worden. Sie spiegeln authentische Situationen aus dem beruflichen Leben wider und regen zur Partnerarbeit und Interaktion an.

Viel Spaß und Erfolg mit Business English for Beginners A1 wünscht Ihnen Autorenteam und Redaktion!

Table of contents

Welcome

❶ Look at the photo. Match the words to the people and things.
Schauen Sie sich das Bild an. Ordnen Sie die Wörter den Menschen und Sachen zu.

1 ☐ laptop   **2** ☐ marker   **3** ☐ whiteboard   **4** ☐ manager

❷ Read the to-do list and underline the words you understand.
Lesen Sie die To-do-Liste und unterstreichen Sie die Wörter, die Sie kennen.

> To do
> - marketing meeting with Sandra's team – 14:00
> - send project update to headquarters
> - briefing with event manager from Erna's Gourmet
> - computer training – 12:00-13:00
> - mail website text to Andrew

❸ Now you: what other English words do you know?
Welche anderen englischen Begriffe kennen Sie?

business

brainstorming

internet

···⟩ **Learning objectives**

You will learn how to:
- introduce yourself and others
- name your job and company

Sie lernen:
- sich und andere vorzustellen
- zu sagen, was Sie beruflich machen und wo Sie arbeiten

Key language:
- job titles
- words for telephone calls

- *I am (not)*
- *he/she is (not)*
- *you/we/they are (not)*
- *a/an*
- *my, your, his, her, its, our, their*
- *'s*
- *What's your name?*
- *Where are you from/based?*
- *What's your job?*

Hello

My name's	=	My name is
I'm	=	I am
What's	=	What is
It's	=	It is

❶ Welcome to Blue Coast Electronics. It is an international company.
Willkommen bei Blue Coast Electronics. Es ist ein internationales Unternehmen.

My name's Maria Santos. What's your name?

I'm Jan Wagner.

🔊02 Listen. Connect the sentence parts.
Hören Sie zu. Verbinden Sie die Satzteile.

1	My name's	**a** project manager with Blue Coast.
2	I'm an	**b** Maria Santos.
3	I'm a	**c** electronics company.
4	It's an	**d** administrative assistant.

a project	**a** vor
a computer	Konsonantlauten
an office	
an assistant	**an** vor Vokallauten

Vor Berufsbezeichnungen steht immer ein Artikel:
I am **an** office worker.
She is **a** software designer.

❷ Read the business card.
Lesen Sie die Visitenkarte.

BLUE COAST
ELECTRONICS

Maria Santos
Administrative assistant

Design department
6822 West Silicon Street
San Francisco, CA 94101 • USA

Tel: +1 (415) 567-3258
E-mail: maria.santos@b-coast.com

Complete Maria's profile on a networking site. Use information from the business card.   Ergänzen Sie Marias Profil in einem sozialen Netzwerk. Verwenden Sie die Informationen aus der Visitenkarte.

Hello. My name's ....[1] I'm with Blue Coast in ....
...................[2], California. It's an international company with offices in the USA and worldwide. I'm an ....[3], an office worker in the ....[4] department.

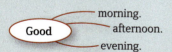

Good — morning.
— afternoon.
— evening.

- Hello, this is .Marina... from .Ford....

- How can I help you?
- Is .Sarah... in the office?

- Just a moment.
- .Jim.., it's .Sally.. for you.

- You're welcome.
- Goodbye/Bye-bye.

❸ 🔊03 Listen to Maria on the telephone. Who is Melanie Kim?
Hören Sie Maria am Telefon zu. Wer ist Melanie Kim?

Maria: Good morning. Blue Coast Electronics. How can I help you?
Jan: Hello Melanie. This is Jan Wagner. I'm a project manager in the Munich office.
Maria: Sorry, this is Maria not Melanie. Maria Santos. I'm the administrative assistant here in the design department.
Jan: Oh sorry, Maria. Is Melanie Kim in the office? She's the new software designer.
Maria: Just a moment, please. Here's Melanie.
Jan: Thank you, Maria.
Maria: You're welcome, Jan.
         Melanie, it's Jan Wagner from Munich for you.

👥 Read the dialogue with a partner.   Lesen Sie den Dialog zu zweit.

4 🔊 04 **Complete the dialogue with the words below. Then listen and check.**
Ergänzen Sie den Dialog mit den untenstehenden Wörtern. Hören Sie dann zu und überprüfen Sie Ihre Antworten.

> 3 ^ 4 5 2
> job · office · project manager · software designer · Welcome

Melanie: Hello. Melanie Kim speaking.

Jan: Hello, Melanie. This is Jan Wagner in the Munich ....¹. How are you?

Melanie: Fine, thanks. And you?

Jan: Fine, thank you. So, today is your first day! ....² to Blue Coast!

Melanie: Thanks, Jan. What's your ....³ in the Munich office?

Jan: I'm a ....⁴ in R&D. You know, the research and development department. And you are a ....⁵, right?

Melanie: That's right.

Complete the information on the business card.
Ergänzen Sie die Informationen auf der Visitenkarte.

BLUE COAST
ELECTRONICS

....
....

Research and development department
Fasanenallee 226
80331 .... • Germany
Tel: +49 89 512 688
E-mail: jan.wagner@b-coast.com

5 **What is the best reaction? Match the sentences.**
Was ist die beste Reaktion? Ordnen Sie die Sätze einander zu.

1 d Good morning.
2 Thank you! c
3 What's your job? e
4 Where are your headquarters? a
5 Mark Smith speaking. b
6 How are you? f

a In the USA.
b Hello. This is Kristin Miller.
c You're welcome!
d Good morning.
e I'm an assistant.
f Fine, thanks. And you?

🔊 05 **Listen and check your answers.** Hören Sie zu und überprüfen Sie Ihre Antworten.

6 👥 **Ask and answer questions about the Blue Coast team.**
Stellen Sie Fragen zu dem Blue Coast team und beantworten Sie sie.

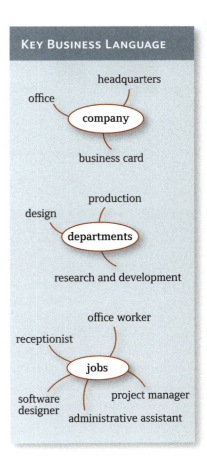

Introductions

1 Complete the texts about Jan and Melanie.
Ergänzen Sie die Texte über Jan und Melanie.

This is Jan Wagner.

He's with Blue Coast Electronics .... [1] Munich.

.... [2] a project manager .... [3] the research

and development department.

.... [4] Melanie Kim.

.... [5] with Blue Coast Electronics .... [6]

San Francisco. .... [7] a software designer

.... [8] the design department.

🔊 **06 Listen and check your answers.**
Hören Sie zu und überprüfen Sie Ihre Antworten.

2 🔊 07 Listen and complete the dialogue.
Hören Sie zu und ergänzen Sie den Dialog.

what's your job at Blue Coast? · what's your name? · Where are you based?

Adam: *Hello. My name's Adam Brown. I'm a production manager here in San Francisco. And* ....

Conor: I'm Conor Griffin.

Adam: So, ...

Conor: I'm a project specialist in the research and development department.

Adam: ....

Conor: I'm based in Munich.

Conor Griffin
Project
specialist
Munich

3 And now you! Und jetzt Sie!

Name:	My name's ....
Company and City:	I'm with .... in ....
Job and Department:	I'm a/an .... in the ....

👥 **Ask a partner.** Fragen Sie einen Partner / eine Partnerin.

> What's your name?

> Which company are you with?

> What's your job?

> Where are you based?

4 **Maria and Melanie are in Maria's office with Peter. Complete the dialogue.**
Maria und Melanie sind mit Peter in Marias Büro. Ergänzen Sie den Dialog.

Maria: Hi Peter. ....¹ are you?

Peter: Not bad, ...². And you?

Maria: ....³. Peter, ...⁴ Melanie Kim, our new software

designer. Melanie, this is Peter. ....⁵ in the production department.

Melanie: Hi Peter. So, ...⁶ your job?

Peter: I'm an administrative assistant.

Maria: Peter's from New York.

Peter: ....⁷ are you from, Melanie?

Melanie: I'm ....⁸ Florida.

🔊**08** **Listen and check your answers.**
Hören Sie zu und überprüfen Sie Ihre Antworten.

5 👥 **Complete the text and read the conversation with a partner.**
Ergänzen Sie die Sätze und lesen Sie das Gespräch zu zweit.

KEY BUSINESS LANGUAGE

Small talk

- How are you?
- Fine / Not bad, thanks.
- And you?
- I'm fine.

- What's your name?
- Which company are you with?
- What's your job?
- Where are you from?
- Where are you based?

◼

Where are you from?	=	Wo sind Sie her?
Where are you based?	=	Wo ist Ihr Standort?

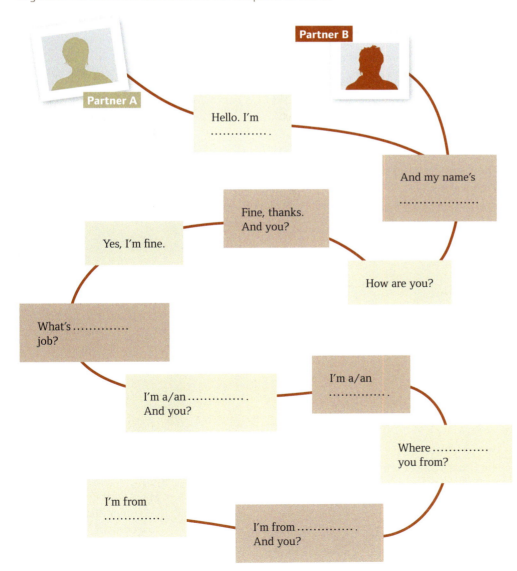

Partner B

Partner A

Hello. I'm ....

And my name's ....

Fine, thanks. And you?

Yes, I'm fine.

How are you?

What's .... job?

I'm a/an .... And you?

I'm a/an ....

Where .... you from?

I'm from ....

I'm from .... And you?

I'm a project manager.

The verb *to be*   Das Verb *to be*

Pronoun		Short form	Negative
I	am	I'm	I'm not
he		he's	he isn't
she	is	she's	she isn't
it		it's	it isn't
we		we're	we aren't
you	are	you're	you aren't
they		they're	they aren't

Melanie? She's the new software designer.
Jan and Conor? They're from the Munich office.

• Die Kurzform wird vor allem in gesprochener Sprache und informeller Schriftsprache verwendet.

Question	Positive answer	Negative answer
Am I …?	Yes, I **am**.	No, I'm **not**.
Is he …?	Yes, he **is**.	No, he **isn't**.
Is she …?	Yes, she **is**.	No, she **isn't**.
Is it …?	Yes, it **is**.	No, it **isn't**.
Are we …?	Yes, we **are**.	No, we **aren't**.
Are you …?	Yes, you **are**.	No, you **aren't**.
Are they …?	Yes, they **are**.	No, they **aren't**.

*Am I right? – Yes, you **are**. / No, you **aren't**.*
*Is he from Munich? – Yes, he **is**. / No, he **isn't**.*

• Nur *Yes* oder *No* hört sich auf Englisch unfreundlich an.

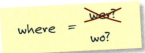

where = ~~wer?~~ wo?

Where are the designers?	**Wo** sind die Designer?
What is your job?	**Was** sind Sie von Beruf?
Who is the project manager?	**Wer** ist der Projektleiter?
Which office is it?	**Welches** Büro ist es?
How are you?	**Wie** geht es Ihnen?

I	**my** job	he	**his** office	we	**our** team
you	**your** job	she	**her** office	you	**your** team
		it	**its** name	they	**their** team

*What's **your** name?*

Blue Coast**'s** offices are in San Francisco.	Die Büros von Blue Coast sind in San Francisco.
Steve is Helena**'s** assistant.	Steve ist Helenas Assistent.

• Mit **'s** wird Besitz und/oder Zugehörigkeit ausgedrückt.

Notes

❶ Fill in a form of *to be*.   Fügen Sie eine Form von *to be* ein.

Hello. My name ....¹ Susan Miller. I ....² with WaterTech. It ....³ an international company. I ....⁴ a software designer in WaterTech's Shanghai office. My two colleagues in the department ....⁵ Huang Li and Chen Yan. They ....⁶ from Beijing.

❷ Correct these statements.   Korrigieren Sie diese Aussagen.

1   Jan Wagner is a software designer.
    No, he isn't. He's a project manager. ....

2   Melanie Kim is a project manager.
    . No, ...

3   Blue Coast's headquarters are in Texas.
    No, they ....

4   Conor Griffin is based in San Francisco.
    No, ...

❸ Ask questions.   Bilden Sie Fragen.

1   Melanie / office worker / in design?   Is Melanie an office worker in design? ....

2   Jan Wagner / software designer?   ....

3   WaterTech / international company?   ....

4   Where / Blue Coast's / headquarters?   ....

5   What / Maria's / job?   ....

👥 **Ask a partner the questions. Answer the questions.**
Stellen Sie die Fragen einem Partner / einer Partnerin. Beantworten Sie die Fragen.

❹ Fill in the right possessive determiner.
Fügen Sie den passenden besitzanzeigenden Begleiter ein.

1   This is Melanie and this is .... assistant Sue.

2   Jan and Conor are based in Germany. .... office is in Munich.

3   The company is an electronics company. .... headquarters are in California.

4   We are in the design department. .... project manager is Martin.

❺ Correct the dialogue. Add apostrophes.
Korrigieren Sie den Dialog. Fügen Sie Apostrophe hinzu.

Anne: Hello Maria. Anne speaking.
Maria: Hello Anne. How are you?
Anne: Im fine, thanks. Is Viktor in the office?
Maria: Viktor?
Anne: Yes, hes a project manager.
Maria: Ah, Viktor. Hes in Jims office. Just a moment, please. Oh no, hes not. Hes here.
Anne: Thank you.

❶ *a* or *an*? *a oder an?*

1	.... assistant	4	.... office worker
2	.... business card	5	.... project manager
3	.... international job	6	.... telephone call

❷ Choose the correct question word: *Who, What, Where, How.* Wählen Sie das richtige Fragewort: *Who, What, Where, How.*

1	.... can I help you?	5	.... are you?
2	...........'s your job?	6	...........'s Maria Santos?
3	.... are you from?	7	.... are your headquarters?
4	...........'s your name?		

👥 **Ask and answer questions 2–7.**
Stellen Sie die Fragen 2–7 und beantworten Sie sie.

❸ Make telephone phrases.
Bilden Sie Ausdrücke am Telefon.

1	*l* Thank	a	are you?
2	☐ How	b	a moment.
3	☐ How can	c	fine, thanks.
4	☐ I'm	d	you.
5	☐ This	e	for you.
6	☐ Just	f	is David.
7	☐ Good	g	welcome.
8	☐ It's Sally	h	I help you?
9	☐ You're	i	afternoon.

❹ 🔊 09 David Pennant from IT Austria is on the telephone to Blue Coast Electronics in San Francisco. Listen and complete the dialogue. David Pennant von IT Austria ist am Telefon mit Blue Coast Electronics in San Francisco. Hören Sie zu und ergänzen Sie den Dialog.

> How are you? • Is • That's right •
> Good morning • I'm fine • Just a
> moment • How can I help you? • This is

Maria: ....[1], Blue Coast Electronics. Maria Santos speaking. ....[2]?

David: Hello. This is David Pennant from IT Austria in Vienna. ....[3] Melanie Kim in the office today?

Maria: ....[4], please.

Melanie: Melanie Kim.

David: Hello, Ms Kim. ....[5] David Pennant from IT Austria in Vienna.

Melanie: Hello, Mr Pennant. ....[6]?

David: ....[7], thanks. So, you are the new software designer in Blue Coast's San Francisco office.

Melanie: ....[8]

👥 **Read the dialogue with a partner.**
Lesen den Dialog zu zweit.

❺ 👥 Ask questions about Jan.
Stellen Sie Fragen über Jan.

Partner A	Wh .... name?	Wh .... job?	Wh .... he based?
Partner B	His .... Jan.	.... project manager.	.... Munich.

Ask a partner.
Fragen Sie einen Partner / eine Partnerin.

Partner A	Wh .... you from?	Wh .... job?	Wh .... name?
Partner B	I'm	I'm	My ....

REAL WORLD

Go to www.xing.com
Look at the people directory. Find XING members.
What are their names, jobs and cities? Tell the class.

Where we are:

	in	out	
Gail Anderson	●	○	
Mark Smith	○	●	AT HOME
Eric Miller	●	○	IN THE CANTEEN
Andrea Wagner	●	○	AT A CONFERENCE
Anna Suarez	●	○	IN A MEETING – ROOM 119
...ily Gupta	○	●	ON A TRAINING COURSE
...rtin Martinez	○	●	OUT OF THE OFFICE TODAY

2

At work

···❯ Learning objectives

❶ Look at the picture. Where are Gail's colleagues?
Schauen Sie sich das Bild an. Wo sind Gails Kollegen und Kolleginnen?

❷ Where are your colleagues?
Wo sind Ihre Kolleginnen und Kollegen?

Name	Place

👥 **Tell your class.**
Berichten Sie Ihrer Klasse.

> Helga is out of the office today

❸ 🔊10 Listen to a phone call. Where is Sandra Li?

a ☐ in Munich   b ☐ in a meeting   c ☐ on a training course

❹ Revision: What telephone phrases can you remember?
Welche Formulierungen am Telefon kennen Sie noch?

· Hello...   · ....   · ....

· ....   · ....

You will learn how to:
· answer a call
· take a message

Sie lernen:
· Anrufe entgegenzunehmen
· Nachrichten aufzunehmen

Key language:
· phrases at work
· the alphabet
· telephone phrases
· numbers

· *Where is/are …?*
· *can/can't*

Where people are

1 **Who is where?**   Wer ist wo?

Bill and Ellen

Martin

Jane and Peter

Eric

Rebecca

Anne

1 ....'s on vacation.

2 ....'s on a training course.

3 ....'s on a business trip.

4 .... are at lunch.

5 .... are in a meeting.

6 ....'s off sick.

holiday 🇬🇧	*Urlaub*
vacation 🇺🇸	*Urlaub*
(public) holiday	*Feiertag*

🔊 11 **Listen and check.**

2 **Where is …? Where are …?**   Wo ist …? Wo sind …?
👥 **Ask a partner.**

> Where **is** Rebecca?

> She**'s** off sick.

> Where **are** Jane and Peter?

> They**'re** in a meeting.

3 🔊 12 **Listen to three phone calls and find the correct information in the boxes.**
Hören Sie drei Anrufe und finden Sie die richtige Information in den Kästchen.

at lunch
at his/her desk

in a meeting
in the office
out of the office

on
— a business trip
— a training course
— the telephone
— holiday 🇬🇧 / vacation 🇺🇸

Jobs
design assistant   design engineer
project manager   project assistant

Where
off sick   on a business trip
on vacation   on a training course

Name	Job	Where is she/he?
Kim Becker	....	....
José Perez	....	....
Amanda Ford	....	....

4 👥 **Where is …? Ask a partner.**

➜ *Partner A: page 63;*   ➜ *Partner B: page 65*

Numbers and spelling

1 🔊 13 **Gail is on the telephone. Listen and do the task.**
Gail ist am Telefon. Hören Sie zu und lösen Sie die Aufgabe.

Gail:	Good afternoon. Blue Coast Electronics. Logistics department. Gail speaking.
Ralf:	Good afternoon. This is Ralf Hillman. Can I speak to Jessica Marks, please?
Gail:	I'm sorry. She's on the telephone at the moment. Can I take a message?
Ralf:	Yes, please. Can she call me back?
Gail:	Of course. What's your phone number, please?
Ralf:	I'm in Berlin. The country code is 49, the area code is 30, and the number is 471 00 26. That's my direct line.
Gail:	OK. Thank you for your call, Mr Hillman.
Ralf:	You're welcome. Goodbye.
Gail:	Goodbye.

Find the English phrases in the phone call.
Finden Sie die englischen Ausdrücke im Telefongespräch.

1 Kann ich bitte … sprechen? ....

2 Kann ich etwas ausrichten? ....

3 Kann sie mich zurückrufen? ....

4 Wie ist Ihre Telefonnummer, bitte? ....

5 Gern geschehen. ....

2 🔊 14 **Listen and repeat.** Hören Sie zu und sprechen Sie nach.

0	zero	**2**	two	**4**	four	**6**	six	**8**	eight
1	one	**3**	three	**5**	five	**7**	seven	**9**	nine

3 **Say the telephone numbers.** Lesen Sie die Telefonnummern laut vor.

a 12 345 67   **b** 559 34 78   **c** 88 03 432   **d** 1-312-667-4000

🔊 15 **Now listen and repeat.**

4 👥 **Ask and answer in small groups.** Fragen Sie und antworten Sie in Kleingruppen.

> What's your telephone number?

> ....

> What's Alex's telephone number?

> His/Her number is …

5 🔊 16 **Listen and repeat the alphabet.** Hören Sie und sprechen Sie das Alphabet nach.

a b c d e f g h i j k l m n o p q r s t u v w x y z

6 **Say these names.** Lesen Sie die Namen laut vor.

■

area code	örtliche Vorwahl
country code	Landesvorwahl
direct line	Durchwahl

■ Nachnamen werden in deutschen Geschäftsbeziehungen häufiger benutzt als in Großbritannien und den USA, wo sich Geschäftspartner oft mit Vornamen ansprechen. Die häufigsten förmlichen Anredeformen in diesen Ländern sind *Mr*, *Mrs* und *Ms*. Ms wird ‚Mizz' ausgesprochen.

■ Sagen Sie bei Telefonnummern immer die einzelnen Zahlen. 0 kann man als *zero* oder *oh* aussprechen. Bei Doppelzahlen wie 55 hört man sowohl *five five* als auch *double five*.

■
Say:
A *capital a*   a *small a*

Taking a message

1 🔊 17 **Listen and decide: is a or b right?** Hören Sie und entscheiden Sie: Ist a oder b richtig?

1 The man's name is
  a James Watson.
  b Jason Watkins.

2 The man's company is
  a Humber and Webber.
  b Humble and Whether.

3 The man's number is
  a 0044-1392-225162.
  b 0044-1392-225612.

2 **Put each phone call in order.**
Bringen Sie jedes Telefongespräch in die richtige Reihenfolge.

1 ☐ Of course. Can you give me your number?
  ☐ Can I speak to Ellen, please?
  ☐ Can she call me back?
  ☐ I'm sorry. She's not in at the moment.

2 ☐ You're welcome. Have a nice day.
  ☐ Thank you for your call.
  ☐ Thank you. You, too.

3 ☐ OK. Fine.
  ☐ I'm in Ireland. The country code is 353 and the number is 1 2894981.
  ☐ Can she call me back?
  ☐ Of course. Can you give me your number, please?

4 ☐ Can I speak to Eric Reed, please?
  ☐ Good morning, Wendy Baxter speaking.
  ☐ Yes, it is. How can I help you?
  ☐ Is this the production department?

🔊 18 **Listen and check.**

3 👥 **Complete the sentences and read the conversation with a partner.**
Ergänzen Sie die Sätze und lesen Sie das Gespräch mit einem Partner / einer Partnerin.

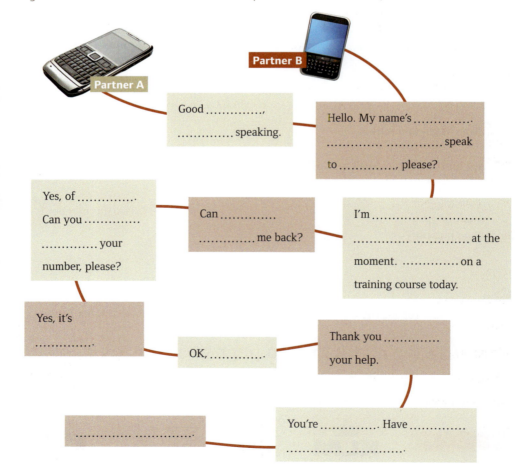

Partner B

Partner A

Good ....,
.... speaking.

Hello. My name's ....
.... speak
to ...., please?

Yes, of ....
Can you ....
.... your
number, please?

Can ....
.... me back?

I'm ....
.... at the
moment. .... on a
training course today.

Yes, it's
....

OK, ...

Thank you ....
your help.

....

You're .... Have ....
....

4 🔊19 👥 **Listen and tick true or false.** Hören Sie zu und markieren Sie richtig oder falsch.

		true	false
1	Sandra West's company is Keynote Systems.	☐	☐
2	Andrew White is in the office.	☐	☐
3	Conor Griffin is in San Francisco.	☐	☐
4	The new brochures are in Conor Griffin's office in Germany.	☐	☐

5 **Fill the gaps with these phrases.** Ergänzen Sie die Lücken mit diesen Ausdrücken.

> Can you spell your name, please? · Can I check that, please? ·
> Can I take a message? · Can I speak to …?

Sandra: Good morning. Keynote Systems, this is Sandra West speaking. How can I help you?

Conor: Good morning, Ms West. This is Conor Griffin from Blue Coast Electronics in Munich. ……………………………………………………[1] Andrew White, please?

Sandra: I'm sorry, Mr Griffin. He can't come to the phone at the moment. ……………………………………………………[2]

Conor: Yes, please. Can he send me the new brochures?

Sandra: Of course. ……………………………………………………[3]

Conor: Certainly, it's C-O-N-O-R G-R-I-F-F-I-N.

Sandra: Ok, I have that. And can you give me your address, please?

Conor: Of course, it's Bergweg 7, 81241 Pasing in Germany.

Sandra: I'm sorry, I can't speak German, so can you spell the name of the street and the town, please?

Conor: Yes, it's Bergweg, that's B-E-R-G-W-E-G, number 7, in Pasing, that's P-A-S-I-N-G.

Sandra: OK. ……………………………………………………[4] It's Mr Conor Griffin, and the address is Bergweg, that's B-E-R-G-W-E-G, number 7, 81241 Pasing, that's P-A-S-I-N-G, in Germany.

Conor: Yes, that's right.

Sandra: OK, thanks. Have a nice day.

Conor: Thank you. You too. Goodbye.

Sandra: You're welcome. Goodbye.

🔊19 **Listen again and check.**

6 🔊20 **Listen and take the message.** Hören Sie zu und schreiben Sie die Nachricht auf.

Call	
Message for:	
From:	Tel:
Company:	
Message:	

7 👥 **Take a message.** Schreiben Sie eine Nachricht.

→ *Partner A: page 63;* → *Partner B: page 65*

KEY BUSINESS LANGUAGE

Taking a message

- Can I take a message?
- Can you give me your name/ address, please?
- Can you repeat that, please?
- Can you spell that, please?
- Can I check that?
- Ok, I have that.

Leaving a message

- Can you take a message, please?
- OK. Fine.
- No thanks, I can call back later.

Call	
Message for:	Andrew White
From:	Conor Griffin
Company:	Blue Coast Electronics
Message:	Send new brochures

Address: Bergweg 7, 81241 Pasing, Germany

Subject and Object pronouns   Subjekt- und Objektpronomen

Subject pronouns	Object pronouns
I	me
you	you
he	him
she	her
it	it
we	us
you	you
they	them

German 'sie' =
she: She's my colleague.
her: Ask Ann, ask her.
they: Ann and Ed? They are here.
them: Ask Ann and Ed, ask them.

*Can **he** call **me** back?*
*Can **I** call **you** back?*
*Can **you** give **him / her** a message?*
*Can **you** give **them** a message?*

---❯ ❶

The verb *can*   Das Verb *can*

I		
You		
He		
She	can / can't	work.
It		
We		
You		
They		

*I **can** speak English, but I **can't** speak Russian.*
*He is on a business trip. I **can** send him an email, but I **can't** call him.*

---❯ ❷

Questions with *can*   Fragen mit *can*

	Can	they	speak English?
	Can	she	come to the meeting?
How	can	I	find you?

Questions Fragen	Short answers Kurzantworten
Can he/she come?	Yes, he/she **can**. / No, he/she **can't**.
Can you speak German?	Yes, I **can**. / No, I **can't**.
Can they come?	Yes, they **can**. / No, they **can't**.

---❯ ❸

Can I help you?

Requests with *can*   Bitten mit *can*

Can I speak to Peter Ferry, please?
Can you spell your name?
Positive answer
Of course. / No problem. / Certainly. / Sure.
Negative answer
I'm sorry, but … / I'm afraid …

ⓘ
· Nach Bitten verwendet man freundliche Erwiderungen wie *of course* oder *I'm sorry, but … .*

---❯ ❹

1 **Fill in the gaps.** Ergänzen Sie die Lücken.

1 **A:** I'm afraid, Mr Garcia's on a training course today.
   B: Can he call .... back, please?
2 **A:** Hi! David Old speaking.
   B: Hello David. I'm in a meeting at the moment. Can I call .... back?
3 **A:** Hello. Susan Hope speaking. Is Bob Martensen in the office?
   B: No, but I can find .... for you.
4 **A:** Good morning. Stuart James speaking. Can I speak to Melissa Kenwood?
   B: I'm sorry. She's out of the office. Can you contact .... on her mobile, please?

2 **Which languages can they speak? Make sentences with *can* and *can't*.**
Welche Sprachen sprechen sie? Bilden Sie Sätze mit *can* und *can't*.

	English	German	Chinese	Spanish
Karin	✔	✔	✗	✔
Mike	✔	✗	✔	✗
Gail	✔	✗	✗	✔

1 Karin can speak English, German and Spanish, but she can't speak Chinese.
2 Mike ....
3 Gail ....
4 Gail and Karin .... Chinese, ... Spanish ....
5 Mike and Gail .... English, ... German ....

3 **Answer the questions with short answers.** Beantworten Sie die Fragen mit Kurzantworten.

1 Can Mike speak Chinese? ....
2 Can Gail speak Chinese? ....
3 Can Mike and Gail speak German? ....
4 Can Karin and Gail speak Spanish? ....

👥 **Now you. Ask a partner.**

Can you speak ...?

No, I can't.

Yes, I can.

4 **Make questions on the telephone.** Bilden Sie Fragen am Telefon.

Can I Can you	spell leave speak repeat check	a your to	message, name, Carlo Rodriguez, that,	please?

1 Can I speak to Carlo Rodriguez, please? ....
2 ....
3 ....
4 ....

Notes

1 **Your colleagues are not in the office. Where are they?**
Ihre Kollegen/Kolleginnen sind nicht im Büro. Wo sind sie?

in · at · on

1 Johannes / a meeting   Johannes.is.in.a.meeting.
2 Gary / a business trip ....
3 Susan / lunch ....
4 Kate & Jim / holiday ....
5 Albert / the telephone ....

👥 **Ask a partner.**

> Can I speak to Johannes, please?

> No, I'm sorry. He's in a meeting.

2 🔊 21 **Listen and write down the order numbers.**
Hören Sie zu und notieren Sie die Auftragsnummern.

1 ....   3 ....
2 ....   4 ....

3 **Complete the dialogue with the phrases from the box.**
Ergänzen Sie den Dialog mit Ausdrücken aus dem Kasten.

Can he · Can I take · Can you give · How can I · That's right. · Can I speak · at lunch · can I check that

Julia: Good morning. PCB Electronics, Julia Redman
speaking. ....¹ help you?

James: Good morning. This is James Gray from Keynote
Systems in Lausanne. ....² to
Jürgen Stenglein, please?

Julia: I'm sorry, Mr Gray. He's ....³ at
the moment. ....⁴ a message?

James: Yes, please. ....⁵ call me back?
It's about my order.

Julia: Of course. ....⁶ me the order
number, please?

James: Yes, it's UFG 733 TC.

Julia: Oh, ...⁷, please? UFG 733 TC?

James: ....⁸

Julia: OK. Thank you for your call, Mr. Gray.

🔊 22 👥 **Listen and check. Then read the dialogue with a
partner.** Lesen Sie dann den Dialog zu zweit.

4 **Put the phone call in the correct order.** Bringen Sie das
Telefongespräch in die richtige Reihenfolge.

a ☐ **Roger:** That's 001 858 742 8155. And what's the
name of your company, please?
b ☐ **Carla:** It's 001 (for the USA), 858 (for San Diego),
then 742 8155.
c ☐ **Roger:** OK. Thank you for calling, Ms Lopez.
Goodbye.
d ☐ **Carla:** Hello. This is Carla Lopez. Is David Hu
there?
e ☐ **Roger:** Certainly, Ms Lopez. Can I have your phone
number, please?
f ☐ **Carla:** Yes, please. It's about our new website. Can
he call me back?
g ☐ **Roger:** Good morning. XMP Software Systems.
Roger Sands speaking. How can I help you?
h ☐ **Roger:** I'm sorry. He's on a business trip. Can I take
a message?
i ☐ **Carla:** PTEC. That's P-T-E-C.

🔊 23 **Listen and check.**

5 👥 **Complete the dialogue. Then read it.** Ergänzen Sie
den Dialog und lesen Sie ihn dann zu zweit.

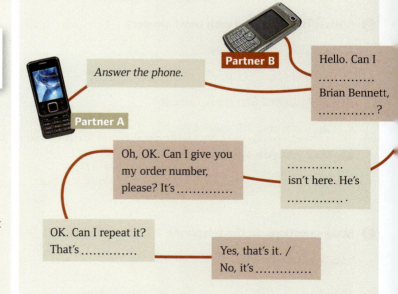

Answer the phone.

Partner A

Partner B

Hello. Can I .... Brian Bennett, ... ?

Oh, OK. Can I give you my order number, please? It's ....

.... isn't here. He's ....

OK. Can I repeat it? That's ....

Yes, that's it. / No, it's ....

Now change roles. Wechseln Sie nun die Rollen.

REAL WORLD
Say these company names: RWE, HSBC, BAE, GKN, BT. Check them on the internet. Which sector are they in?

Around the company

⋯⫶ Learning objectives

1 **What can you see in the picture?**
Was sehen Sie im Bild?

A photocopier.

A plant.

2 🔊24 **Listen and number these things in the order you hear them.**
Hören Sie zu und nummerieren Sie diese Sachen in der Reihenfolge, in der Sie sie hören.

book .... computer .... mobile phone .... plant .l.................

chair .... photocopier .... monitor .... water cooler ....

coffee machine .... desk .... mouse .... window ....

Which things can't you see in the photo?

3 **What is in your office?** Was befindet sich in Ihrem Büro?

I have: .a computer...

4 **Revision. Are the sentences true or false?** Sind die Sätze richtig oder falsch?

		true	false
1	Blue Coast's headquarters are in New York.	☐	☐
2	Jan Wagner is a project manager.	☐	☐
3	Jan's office is in Munich.	☐	☐

You will learn how to:
· greet visitors
· name things in the office
· say where things are

Sie lernen:
· Besucher zu begrüßen
· Bürogegenstände zu benennen
· zu sagen, wo sich etwas
  befindet

Key language
· phrases for meeting and
  greeting
· office equipment
· expressions of place

· *there is/are*
· plurals
· *to have*

Meeting and introducing people

❶ Complete the dialogue.

Nice to meet you too. · Thank you. · That's right.

Jessica: Excuse me. Are you Jan Wagner?

Jan: ....
Jessica: I'm Jessica Marks. Nice to meet you.

Jan: ....
Jessica: Welcome to California.

Jan: ....
Jessica: Can I take your coat?
Jan: Thank you. Here you are.

🔊25 **Now listen and check.**

❷ Greet a partner. Use ❶ for help.
Begrüßen Sie einen Partner/eine Partnerin mit Hilfe von ❶.

❸ 🔊26 👥 Listen to the conversation. Then read it with a partner.

Jessica: Jan, can I introduce you to Martina Williams? Martina is in the logistics department. Martina, this is Jan Wagner from our Munich office.
Jan: Nice to meet you, Ms Williams.
Martina: Nice to meet you too. Please call me Martina.

❹ 👥 Now you. Greet a friend, then introduce a new person.
Begrüßen Sie eine(n) Bekannte(n), stellen Sie dann eine neue Person vor.

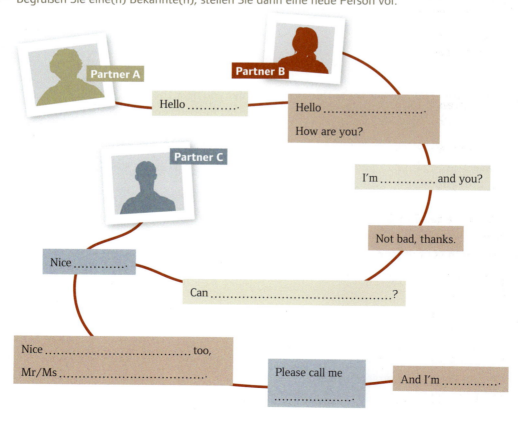

Partner A — Hello ....

Partner B — Hello ....
How are you?

I'm .... and you?

Not bad, thanks.

Partner C

Nice ....

Can ....?

Nice .... too,
Mr/Ms ....

Please call me ....

And I'm ....

KEY BUSINESS LANGUAGE

Meeting and greeting

· Excuse me.
· Are you *Inq..*? Yes I am.
· I'm *Susanne*.
· Nice/Pleased to meet you.
· Nice/Pleased to meet you too.
· Welcome to *Blue Coast*
· Can I take your coat?
· Thank you. Here you are.
· Please call me *Max*.......

Can I show you around?

❶ 🔊27 Listen to the dialogue, then read it with a partner.

Jessica: Can I show you around?

Jan: Yes, please. Head office is so big. Our Munich office is small.

Jessica: Well, we have a production department here at headquarters. Look, here's the floor plan. We're here in reception. And this is the production area, this yellow area over here on the left.

❷ 🔊28 Listen. Tick the departments that Jessica mentions.
Hören Sie zu. Kreuzen Sie die Abteilungen an, die Jessica nennt.

What colour are the departments that Jessica mentions? And the departments that she doesn't mention? Welche Farbe haben die Abteilungen, die Jessica nennt? Und die Abteilungen, die sie nicht nennt?

❸ 🔊29 Listen to the rest of the dialogue and tick the phrases that you hear.
Hören Sie den Rest des Dialogs und kreuzen Sie die Ausdrücke an, die Sie hören.

☐ Can you show me …?
☐ This way, please.
☐ Can you tell me where … is/are?

☐ It's/They're along here.
☐ On the left.
☐ On the right.

❹ 🔊30 Listen and fill in the plan with the words in the box. There are two you don't need. Vervollständigen Sie den Übersichtsplan mit den Wörtern im Kasten. Es gibt zwei, die Sie nicht brauchen.

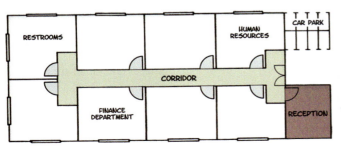

administration ·
conference room ·
logistics · purchasing
production · sales ·
warehouse

> ■ Im Englischen gibt es viele Wörter für das WC. Das Gebräuchlichste ist *restroom*. In England werden Ihnen auch die Wörter *WC* und *toilet* begegnen. In Nordamerika spricht man von *bathroom*.

KEY BUSINESS LANGUAGE

· Can I show you (a)round?
· Can I give you a tour?
· Yes, please.
· This way, please.
· Can you show me …?
· Can you tell me where … is/are?
· along here
· on the left/right
· next to …
· between … and …
· opposite …

Describing locations

① 🔊 31 **Listen to the conversation. Tick the things which are at Blue Coast's headquarters and/or the Munich office.** Hören Sie sich das Gespräch an. Setzen Sie einen Haken neben die Dinge, die es in der Zentrale von Blue Coast bzw. der Außenstelle in München gibt.

	San Francisco office	Munich office
water cooler	☐	☐
childcare centre	☐	☐
sports facilities	☐	☐
staff restaurant	☐	☐
shop	☐	☐
staff car park/parking lot	☐	☐

■

car park 🇬🇧   Parkplatz

parking lot 🇺🇸   Parkplatz

KEY BUSINESS LANGUAGE

human resources department

production area

logistics department

warehouse

locations

purchasing department

reception area

finance department

sales department

Office and conference room

chair	projector
desk	wall
flip chart	whiteboard
power point	window

---

② **Now you. Ask a partner.**

Is there a … ?

Yes, **there is.**

No, **there isn't.**

Are there any … ?

Yes, **there are.**

No, **there aren't.**

③ 🔊 32 **There is a visitor's office at Blue Coast headquarters. Listen to the conversation and fill the gaps.** In der Blue Coast Zentrale gibt es ein Büro für Firmenbesucher. Hören Sie das Gespräch und ergänzen Sie die Lücken.

Jessica: So, Jan. Here's our visitor's office.

Jan: Very nice.

Jessica: Yes. You have a computer with high-speed internet ....on...........¹ the desk, and the printer is here on this small table ....² the desk. There's extra paper for the printer ....³ on the left.

behind · in front of · in the corner · next to · ~~on~~ · under

Jan: OK.

Jessica: There are power points ....⁴ the desk here.

Jan: Ah yes. Good.

Jessica: OK, then on the wall ....⁵ the desk is the control panel for the air conditioning.

Jan: Great.

Jessica: I think that's all.

Jan: What's that document on the desk ....⁶ the phone?

Jessica: Oh, that's the head office list – it has all the phone numbers and email addresses.

④ **Now you. Tick what is true for you, your office and your company.**

1 ☐ I have air conditioning in my office.   4 ☐ We have a conference room.
2 ☐ I have blinds in my office.   5 ☐ The conference room has a projector.
3 ☐ I have a flip chart in my office.   6 ☐ It has a whiteboard too.

⑤ **Look at these pictures of a conference room. Where is the loudspeaker?**

The loudspeaker is …	in the middle of …	… the ceiling.
	on …	… the window.
	opposite …	… the table.

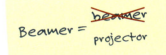
Beamer = ~~beamer~~ projector

KEY BUSINESS LANGUAGE

Describing locations

- It is …   between
- They are …   next to
- There is a … at the back (of)
- There are … at the front (of)
              in front of
              in the corner (of)
              in the middle (of)
              on
              on the right/left
              opposite
              under

⑥ 🔊33 **Listen and read the conversation. Then say what is where.**

Jessica: So, here's the conference room, Jan. I think it's perfect for your presentation. As you can see, the conference table has ten chairs. And there's a laptop and a pointer for presentations.

Jan: Great. And where's the projector?

Jessica: It's on the ceiling.

Jan: Ah! I see.

Jessica: There are blinds at the windows. And there is a whiteboard on the wall opposite the windows.

Jan: OK.

Jessica: And there are 10 power points for laptops in the middle of the table.

Jan: Oh yes. That's very good. Er… I can't see loudspeakers.

Jessica: There are mini-loudspeakers here at the side.

Jan: Of course. Sorry. Can we have a video conference here?

Jessica: Certainly. The technology is installed and the microphones are here in the middle of the table, next to the power points. So, is everything OK?

Jan: Yes, thank you.

What?	Where?
1 projector	a in the middle of the table
2 loudspeakers	b on the ceiling
3 power points	c in the corner of the room
4 whiteboard	d at the back of the room
5 microphones	e on the wall opposite the windows
	f at the side

KEY BUSINESS LANGUAGE

Asking questions

- Is there …?/Are there any …?
- Where is/are …?
- Where can I …?
- Can you show me …, please?

⑦ 👥 **Describe a conference room.** Beschreiben Sie einen Konferenzraum.

➡ *Partner A: page 63;* ➡ *Partner B: page 65*

There is / There are   Es gibt

es gibt = ~~it gives~~ there is/are

Singular Einzahl	Plural Mehrzahl
There is one room. **There's** one room.	**There are** two rooms.

Questions Fragen	Short Answers Kurzantworten
Is there a conference room?	Yes, **there is.** / No, **there isn't.**
Are there any brochures?	Yes, **there are.** / No, **there aren't.**

ⓘ
· Fragen Sie nach mehreren Sachen mit
Are there any …?

⋯⟶ ❶ ❷ ❸

The plural of nouns   Nomen im Plural

one country

Plural of most nouns: s

one room	two room**s**
one brochure	two brochure**s**
one office	two office**s**

Nouns ending in -s, -ss, -sh, -ch, -x: es

one address	two address**es**
one lunch	two lunch**es**
one fax	two fax**es**

Nouns ending in consonant + y: ies

one country	two countr**ies**
one copy	two cop**ies**
one company	two compan**ies**

countries

Irregular plural   Unregelmäßiger Plural

one child	two child**ren**	one man	two m**e**n
one woman	two wom**e**n	one person	two **people**

⋯⟶ ❹

The verb *to have*   Das Verb *to have*

I	**have**
you	**have**
he	**has**
she	**has**
it	**has**
we	**have**
you	**have**
they	**have**

*I **have** two whiteboards in my office.*
*She **has** nice colleagues.*
*We **have** two offices, one in Munich and one in London.*

⋯⟶ ❺

1 Complete the sentences with *there is/are*. Ergänzen Sie die Sätze mit *there is/are*.

To: hering@construction.co.uk
Subject: My new office

This is a picture of my new office. ....¹ two desks at the back of the room, and ....² a table for meetings at the front. ....³ four comfortable chairs round the table. The office is nice. ....⁴ two big windows, at the back and at the side, and ....⁵ a nice big plant too.

Notes

2 What's in your company? Tick the boxes.

☐ restroom for visitors   ☐ warehouse   ☐ sports facilities
☐ conference rooms   ☐ lifts   ☐ blinds at the windows

Make sentences with *There is a / There isn't a / There are / There aren't any*

....
....
....
....

3 Ask a partner questions about his/her office and department. Then tell the class.

☐ copiers   ☐ flip chart   ☐ printer
☐ whiteboard   ☐ plants   ☐ facilities for video conferences

Are there any copiers in your department?

No, **there aren't.**

Is there a flip chart in your office?

No, **there isn't.**

There isn't a flip chart in Bernd's office.

4 Write the plural.

address ....   department ....   office ....

chair ....   businessman ....   day ....

company ....   floor plan ....   businesswoman ....

5 Complete the sentences with *have* and *has*.

Dubai Construction
Logistics department

We ....¹ two seminar rooms.

The sales manager ....² one next to her office, and

they ....³ one in the administration department. That

room ....⁴ video conference facilities.

1 👥 **Introduce yourself and a new person.**
Stellen Sie sich und eine andere Person vor.

> Hello ... Can I introduce you to ... ?

> Nice to meet you too.

> Nice to meet you.

2 **Underline the correct expression.**
Unterstreichen Sie den richtigen Ausdruck.

1 It's sunny today and there aren't any blinds at the window / on the wall . Isn't this a problem?

2 I can write the web address on the whiteboard / projector for you.

3 There are ten power points in the ceiling / floor .

4 I can't see my PowerPoint presentation. Is the projector / loudspeaker on?

5 Is there a pen / pointer for the projector?

6 Excuse me! Where's the paper for the printer / projector ?

3 **What can you see in your classroom? Ask and answer, then write sentences with words from the box.** Was können Sie in Ihrem Klassenraum sehen? Befragen Sie sich gegenseitig, dann schreiben Sie Sätze mit den Wörtern aus dem Kasten.

> Is there ...?

> Are there any ...?

> No, there aren't.

> Yes, there are four ...

> on the right · on the left ·
> at the front · in the corner · at the back ·
> in front of · next to · in the middle

There is a flip chart on the right of the room.

....

....

....

....

....

....

....

4 🔊 34 **A visitor gets a tour. Listen and complete the floor plan.** Eine Besucherin erhält einen Rundgang. Hören Sie zu und ergänzen Sie den Übersichtsplan.

> finance department · garden · human resources ·
> logistics · meeting room · purchasing department ·
> sales department · WC

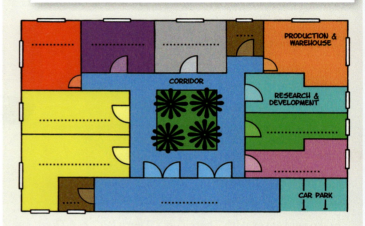

5 **Complete the dialogue.**

> between · in the · next to ·
> in front of · on the right · left

Maria: So, this is our new building.
Visitor: Very nice.
Maria: Here's a floor plan of the company. We're here

....[1] reception area.
Visitor: Yes, right.
Maria: Here are the meeting rooms. They're on the

..............[2]. They're ....[3] the finance department. It's red on the plan.
Visitor: Mmmm.
Maria: The sales department is here, in the corner

....[4] you.
Visitor: That's great, thanks. Where is the restroom?

Maria: The restroom? There's one ....[5] the purchasing department and the production area.

They're here ....[6]

👥 **Check your answers. Then read the dialogue with a partner.**

REAL WORLD

Draw a plan of your office or company. Tell the class.

Colleagues and companies

···▸ **Learning objectives**

❶ Look at the sketch maps. What are the countries? What other countries can you name?

Australia	China	Germany	Japan	Sweden
Austria	Denmark	India	The Netherlands	Switzerland
Brazil	Finland	Ireland	Portugal	The United
Canada	France	Italy	Spain	Kingdom

❷ Complete this list of nationalities for the countries in ❶.

Ending -(i)an		Ending -ese	Ending -ish	Other
Australian	Germ...	Chinese	Danish	British
Austr...	Ind...	Japan...	Finn...	Dutch
Brazil...	Ital...	Portugu...	Ir...	French
Canad...			Span...	Swiss
			Swed...	

❸ What can you say about these companies? Where are they based? What other companies do you know?

You will learn how to:
- talk about yourself
- talk about your company
- exchange information

Sie lernen:
- über sich selbst zu sprechen
- über Ihr Unternehmen zu sprechen
- Informationen auszutauschen

Key language:
- countries and nationalities
- company facts
- business cards

- *Where are you from?*
- *I/You/We/They work*
- *He/She works*
- *Where do you/they work?*
- *Where does he/she work?*

Business contacts

1 **Match the parts.**

1 ☐ A colleague   a buys from you.
2 ☐ A customer   b sells to you.
3 ☐ A supplier   c works with you.

🔊35 **Now listen to three conversations and complete these profiles. Use words from 1**

■ Nationalitäten und Sprachen werden immer groß geschrieben.

2
Amina Abbad

She's a Dutch ....
She sells parts for mobile phones to Blue Coast.

1
Jan Wagner

He's .German...... He works for Blue Coast. He's a

....
of Jessica's.

3
Stephan Camenzind

He's Swiss. He buys computers from Blue Coast. He's a big European

....

2 **Complete the texts with words from the boxes.**

1

Frank Lewis

| buys · does · has |

Frank Lewis is Canadian. He ....[1] a company in Montreal. He ....[2] cell phones from Blue Coast. He's a good customer. Blue Coast ....[3] a lot of business with him.

| makes · sells · works |

Isobel Lennox is British, she's from Scotland. She ....[1] for Hightime Electronics in Aberdeen. The company ....[2] office equipment. Hightime Electronics ....[3] to Blue Coast, but also to companies in Europe.

2

Isobel Lennox

| does · has · produces · supplies |

3

Yen Lee

Yen Lee is one of Blue Coast's Chinese contacts. His company, RMT Electronics, ...[1] three factories in China. The company ....[2] electronic components for Blue Coast. It ....[3] all Blue Coast's cell phone components. The people at Blue Coast say that Yen Lee's company ....[4] a very good job.

🔊36 **Listen and check.**

Exchanging information

❶ 🔊37 **Listen to Claire and Isobel. Highlight the *Key Business Language* in the dialogue.**

Claire Gerber
Hardware specialist
Purchasing department

Specialist Office Equipment GmbH
Werkstr. 68, Zurich 8001, Switzerland
Tel.: + 41 44 2668952, Email: claire_gerber@soe.ch

Isobel Lennox
Sales representative
Hardware department

Hightime Electronics Ltd
23 Deansgrange Road
Aberdeen AB22
Scotland

Tel.: +44 1224 589689
Email: i.lennox@hightime.co.uk

Claire: Hello, I'm Claire Gerber from Specialist Office Equipment in Zurich.

Isobel: Nice to meet you. I'm Isobel Lennox from Hightime Electronics. What does your company do?

Claire: We produce office equipment. Here's my card.
I'm a hardware specialist in the purchasing department of our company.

Isobel: That's interesting. I work in the hardware department of my company. We supply office equipment too. We specialize in video conference equipment.

Claire: Really? We need a new supplier. Can I call you for more information?

Isobel: Of course. No problem. Here's my card.

Claire: That's great. Thanks very much.

Isobel: But I have a new email address.
It's now lennox underscore isobel at hightime dot co dot uk.

Exchanging information

- I'm … and work for …
- I'm a … in the … department.
- That's interesting.
- What does your company do?
- We make/sell/supply …
- Can I call/email you for more information?
- You can call/email me for more information.
- Here's my card.

■ Company types

plc	Inc./Corp.	AG
Ltd	Inc./Corp.	GmbH

❷ Look at the box on the right. Say these email addresses.

To: sam.parker_west@hpl-systems.com

To: martina.essert@reveillert.co.uk

👥 **Now you. Tell a partner your email address.**

❸ 🔊38 **Melanie Kim is on the phone to four suppliers. Listen and write down the email or website address.**

1 ....

2 ....

3 ....

4 ....

■ Email addresses

.	dot	-	hyphen/dash
@	at	_	underscore

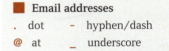

You and your company

1 Read the email and answer the true-false questions.

Subject: Special offer

Dear Mr Lebedev,
First let me introduce myself. My name's Sandra Butler and I work in the marketing department of Blue Coast, the international electronics company. We have our headquarters in the US, but we operate worldwide. Here in Europe the company has operations in Munich, Amsterdam and Poznań, Poland. In Munich they do R&D. The Polish factory produces modules for Blue Coast hardware, and here in Amsterdam we coordinate European sales and marketing.

Are these statements true or false?

		true	false
1	Blue Coast operates worldwide.	☐	☐
2	It has a European office in London.	☐	☐
3	Sandra works in the production department.	☐	☐
4	In Amsterdam they do design work.	☐	☐

2 Match the sentence beginnings and endings.

1 ☐ Our company's headquarters   **a** are based in China.
2 ☐ We have offices   **b** does PR work.
3 ☐ The main suppliers   **c** in Munich and Amsterdam.
4 ☐ My department   **d** are in San Francisco.

KEY BUSINESS LANGUAGE

Company facts

Offices
- Our headquarters are in …
- We have offices/branches in …
- We operate worldwide.
- We are active in … countries.

Products

manufacture
sell
make
We
produce
supply

Customers & suppliers
- The company's main customers/suppliers are …

Company

My department — organizes
— plans
— coordinates

3 Complete this fact sheet for your company.

My company: ....

♦ My company's headquarters are in ....

♦ We have offices in ....

♦ The main suppliers are ....

♦ The main customers are ....

♦ My department ....

4 Write an email like the one in exercise **1**.

Subject: Invitation

Dear …
First let me introduce myself. My name's …

5 🔊 **39** **Read and listen to part of a presentation and complete the fact sheet.**

> Good morning and welcome to our headquarters.
> Let me introduce myself. My name is Juliana Freitag. I'm the
> Sales Manager here at Bautechnik. We are a large company. We have
> our headquarters here in Ulm and offices in Hamburg, Frankfurt and Leipzig.
> But we are also a global company with offices in other parts of Europe,
> North America, India, China, Brazil, Turkey and Russia. We have …

Name and job:	....¹
Name of company and headquarters:	Bautechnik GmbH, Ulm ....
Offices in:	....
	....²

6 🔊 **40** **The audience asks Juliana Freitag some questions about her presentation. Match each question with an answer. Then listen and check.**

1 ▢ What does your factory in the Netherlands produce?

2 ▢ How many offices do you have in China?

3 ▢ How many employees are there in the Hamburg office?

4 ▢ What does your supplier in Jakarta supply?

5 ▢ How many products does your company have on its website?

6 ▢ How many suppliers do you have in South America?

a Wood. 20,000 cubic metres a year.

b Three – no, four. We have a new supplier in Buenos Aires now.

c We have two.

d Over 2,000.

e It makes windows and doors for the European market.

f There are ten. It's a small office.

7 **Put the words in each question in the correct order.**

1 do / work in / you / what department / ? ....

2 you / in your department / have / how many colleagues / do / ? ....

3 your company / what / make or sell / does / ? ....

4 are / how many departments / there / in your company / ? ....

5 in Germany / have / your company / does / how many offices / ? ....

6 are / your main customers / where / ? ....

Now ask your partner the questions.

8 👥 **Ask a partner about his/her company.**

➜ *Partner A: page 64;* ➜ *Partner B: page 66*

▨ **Achtung: falsche Freunde!**

Wörter, die im Deutschen und im Englischen ähnlich sind, haben nicht immer eine ähnliche Bedeutung. Achten Sie auf die folgenden Wörter.

factory	*Fabrik*
fabric	*Stoff/Gewebe*
get/receive	*bekommen*
become	*werden*
boss	*Chef*
chef	*Küchenchef*
check	*kontrollieren*
control	*beherrschen*
mobile phone 🇬🇧	*Handy*
cell phone 🇺🇸	*Handy*
handy	*praktisch*

Simple present Einfache Gegenwart

I	**work**	in Munich.
You	**work**	in Munich.
He	**works**	in Munich.
She	**works**	in Munich.
It	**works**	in Munich.
We	**work**	in Munich.
You	**work**	in Munich.
They	**work**	in Munich.

- 3. Person Singular: das Verb bekommt ein **s**.
- Wir verwenden die einfache Gegenwart, um über Fakten oder Routinehandlungen zu sprechen.

*I **come** from Germany.*
*You **know** Gregory.*
*He **works** as an assistant.*
*She **lives** in Chicago.*
*Her company **produces** electronic components.*
*We **produce** office equipment.*
*They **supply** us.*

> He, she, it – das s muss mit.

Questions Fragen

What	**do**	I	**do?**
What	**do**	you	**make?**
When	**does**	he	**start?**
When	**does**	she	**start?**
When	**does**	it	**start?**
Where	**do**	we	**work?**
Where	**do**	you	**work?**
Where	**do**	they	**work?**

- I/you/we/they: **do**
- he/she/it: **does**
- Nach *does* wird kein **s** an das Verb angehängt.

*When **do** I give my presentation?*
*Where **do** you produce your components?*
*What **does** Martin do?*
*How many colleagues **does** she have?*
*What **does** the company produce?*
*Where **do** we start the tour?*
*Why **do** they produce modules in Ireland?*

❶ Read this profile from a company website. Fill in the correct form of the verb.

I ....¹ (work) for PlanTech in the Sales Department here at the

headquarters in Dundee, Scotland. PlanTech ....² (design) and

........................³ (manufacture) modules for PCs, mobile phones and many other

electrical products. We ....⁴ (have) five major customers in Europe and one

in the USA. Our American costumers ....⁵ (be) Blue Coast Electronics. It

........................⁶ (buy) modules for its MP3 players and portable DVD players from us.

❷ Read some more information about PlanTech. Fill the gaps with these words.

> His assistants · He · It · PlanTech · PlanTech's European clients ·
> The Head of Sales · They · They

........................¹ has 65 employees at its headquarters in Dundee and 40 in its factory in

Stirling. ....² has a large Sales Department with 20 managers and assistants.

........................³ all work in Dundee. ....⁴ is Stuart McPhee.

........................⁵ often travels to California and Vancouver. ....⁶ are Laura

Walsh and Patrick Dunbar. ....⁷ often go with him on his trips to North

America. ....⁸ are based in Germany, Finland, Sweden, Poland and Romania.

❸ Write questions.

1   Laura Walsh works in <u>Aberdeen</u>. *Where does Laura Walsh work?* ....

2   The production workers work in <u>Stirling</u>. *Where* ....

3   PlanTech has <u>five major clients</u> in Europe. *How many* ....

4   It manufactures <u>electronic components</u>. *What* ....

5   Patrick Dunbar works in the <u>Sales Department</u>. *Where* ....

6   Blue Coast buys <u>modules for its MP3 players</u>. *What* ....

7   PlanTech's major European client is based in <u>Finland</u>. *Where* ....

❹ A client contacts RDD, a company in the car industry. Complete the client's questions with *do, does, is, are*.

1   Where .... the company based?

2   How many suppliers .... the company have in South America?

3   What .... the company sell?

4   Where .... the company's offices in the USA?

5   How many products .... the company have on its website?

6   What .... the company's two Chinese suppliers manufacture?

7   Which products .... the company make for the US market?

8   Where .... the company's Eastern European factories?

1 **Match the people and what they do.**

1 ☐ My colleague   **a** make products for us.
2 ☐ Our suppliers   **b** is my manager.
3 ☐ Our customers   **c** works with me.
4 ☐ My boss   **d** buy products from us.

👥 **Ask a partner.**

Who is your best supplier / best customer?
Where are they based?

Where are they based?

Who is your best customer?

My best customer is a company called Lenvox.

They're based in London. They're a British company.

2 🔊 41 **Listen and write down the phone numbers and email addresses.**

1 ....
2 ....
3 ....
4 ....

3 **Fill in your information.**

Company name
....

Office number   ....
Mobile number   ....
Email address   ....

👥 **Ask a partner.**

4 **Write the questions and sentences.**

1 does / your / what / do / company?

....

2 information / can / I / call / you / more / for?

....

3 card / my / here's

....

4 department / the / I'm / sales / in

....

5 me / let / first / myself / introduce

....

5 **Complete the dialogue with words from the box.**
Ergänzen Sie den Dialog mit Wörtern aus dem Kasten.

> am a project manager · are you from · Austrian ·
> business card · Italian · Nice to meet you. ·
> that's interesting · work for

Pia: Hello, Peter. I'm Pia. ....
....[1].

Peter: Hello, Pia. It's nice to meet you too. Where are you
from?

Pia: I'm ....[2]. I ....[3]
Abarth in Bologna. Where ....
....[4]?

Peter: I'm ....[5]. I come from Linz and
I ....
.................[6] with Profone.

Pia: Oh, ...[7]. Here's my
....[8].

👥 **Now read the dialogue with a partner.**

6 **Match the sentence parts.**

1 ☐ Blue Coast Electronics buys
2 ☐ Blue Coast Electronics sells
a electronic parts from suppliers.
b computers and mobile phones to customers.

3 ☐ Blue Coast Electronics makes
4 ☐ Blue Coast Electronics does
a business with people around the world.
b my favourite electronic products.

5 ☐ Yen's factory does
6 ☐ Yen's factory makes
a electronic components.
b a good job.

REAL WORLD

Where are your business partners based?
Write their country and nationality.

Work schedules

⋯⟩ Learning objectives

**❶ What do you do regularly in your job?
See the photos and box for ideas.**

make coffee · send emails ·
go to meetings · meet visitors ·
listen to my iPod · call customers ·
watch YouTube · write a newsletter

> I make coffee
> every day.

You will learn how to:
· talk about work
· talk about free time

Sie lernen:
· über die Arbeit zu sprechen
· über die Freizeit zu sprechen

❷ 👥 Brainstorming: Name other activities.

at work: *go on a training course*...

free time: *do yoga*...

Key language:
· numbers & times
· days of the week
· activities at work
· free-time activities

· I/You/We/They don't work
· He/She/It doesn't work
· Do I/you/we/they work …?
· Does he/she/it work …?
· How often?
· usually, sometimes, never
· I like/love doing …

**❸ 🔊42 Four people talk about what they do in their lunch hour. Who goes where?
Who eats what? What does each person do? Listen and write 1, 2, 3 or 4 in the boxes.**

Where does he/she eat?	What does he/she eat?	What does he/she do?
☐ in his/her office	☐ a soup/pasta	☐ listens to hip-hop music
☐ at home	☐ a salad	☐ reads the newspaper
☐ in the staff restaurant	☐ a hot lunch	☐ talks to colleagues
☐ in a bread shop	☐ a sandwich	☐ listens to the radio

Routines

1 **Put the events in the correct order.**

a ▢ At quarter past nine my colleagues and I usually have breakfast together.

b ▢ Before I go home, I check my emails one last time. I get between 30 and 40 emails a day.

c ▢ I often have lunch in the canteen.

d ▢ But I sometimes work overtime. I don't like doing it.

e ▢ I start work early, at seven or half past seven.

f ▢ I switch on my computer and check my emails. That's the first thing.

g ▢ It's usually about quarter to four when I switch off my computer and leave.

> ■ Es gibt zwei Möglichkeiten, über diese Zeiten zu reden.
>
> | :15 | fifteen | | quarter past |
> |-----|---------|---|--------------|
> | :30 | thirty | or | half past |
> | :45 | forty-five | | quarter to |
>
> 9:15 nine fifteen / quarter past nine
> 9:30 nine thirty / half past nine
> 9:45 nine forty-five / quarter to ten

> *Im Englischen zählt man die halbe Stunde **nach** der vollen Stunde.*
>
> 16:30
> 4:30   half past four
>
> 17:30
> 5:30   half past five

2 🔊43 **Match these responses to the sentences in 1. Then listen and check.**

1 I can't do overtime, I have a family at home.

2 I don't have a breakfast break.

3 That's a lot. I get about 15 a day.

4 I don't like our canteen. I usually have lunch at my desk.

5 Really? I don't start before nine!

6 That's my first thing too.

7 That's early, but you start early of course. I don't finish before five thirty or six.

👥 Now say the sentences in 1 and the responses with a partner.

3 🔊44 **Listen and repeat the numbers.**

11	eleven	16	sixteen	21	twenty-one	60	sixty
12	twelve	17	seventeen	22	twenty-two	70	seventy
13	thirteen	18	eighteen	30	thirty	80	eighty
14	fourteen	19	nineteen	40	forty	90	ninety
15	fifteen	20	twenty	50	fifty	100	a hundred

4 🔊45 **Listen and write the numbers.**

a ....   c ....   e ....   g ....

b ....   d ....   f ....   h ....

5 What time is it?

It's ...am /
in the morning.

It's ...pm / in the
afternoon.

6 Read the text and match the activities to the times below.

Blue Coast has a competition – people can win a holiday in Barbados. They write about their day and their Blue Coast smartphone. This is James Manning's entry.

My Blue Coast smartphone is my lifeline to my girlfriend Emma, because I don't have a normal day, and it's the only way to keep in touch with her. She works in an office from nine to five and does the usual office tasks: she sorts the post, makes photocopies, calls customers, shows visitors round, writes emails – and is home at 6 pm. But my routine is quite different. I work for a sandwich production company. Our customers want really fresh products in the supermarket in the morning, so I start work at 10 in the evening and I finish at 6.30 in the morning. I have one break, between 1.30 and 2 in the morning. I have a cup of tea and sometimes an apple or a banana. When my working day ends, I go home and make breakfast for Emma and me. We always have breakfast together at 8 before she goes to work at half past. Then I usually go online to read the news. Later in the morning I sometimes go to the shops, and I often work on my hobby from 11 to 12: I update the website of our local sports club. Lunchtime is the end of my day. I go to bed every day at 12.30, and I sleep until about 6.30 in the evening. For me the evening is the start of the day. I have a meal with Emma and we watch TV. Then at 9.15 in the evening I leave the house. I stay in touch with Emma until she goes to bed – my Blue Coast smartphone really is my lifeline.

James Manning

Time		Activity	
1	6.30 am	a	He leaves home.
2	8 am to 8.30 am	b	He has an evening meal with Emma.
3	11 am to midday	c	He finishes work.
4	12.30 pm to 6.30 pm	d	He starts work.
5	6.30 pm to 7 pm	e	He has a cup of tea.
6	9.15 pm	f	He updates the sports club website.
7	10 pm	g	He sleeps.
8	1.30 am to 2 am	h	He has breakfast.

7 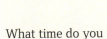 Ask a partner.

What time do you	get to work?
	have a break?
	have lunch?
	finish work?
	get home?
	go to bed?

Usually at
about eleven.

At nine o'clock.

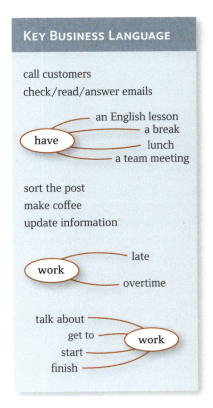

KEY BUSINESS LANGUAGE

call customers
check/read/answer emails

have — an English lesson
— a break
— lunch
— a team meeting

sort the post
make coffee
update information

work — late
— overtime

talk about
get to — work
start
finish

Work-life balance

❶ ◖⬭46 Listen and take notes.

Mary Thompson works for a company called Capital City in London. She is with her friend and ex-colleague Anna from Blue Coast. Listen to their conversation and complete the table.

Good work-life balance	Problems
• .She.always.has.a.free.weekend..............	• .She.always.starts.work.very.early.and.......
•	• ....
•	• ....

■ In Zeitplänen und Kalendern wird die Uhrzeit *16:30* geschrieben. Im gesprochenen Alltagsenglisch redet man von *4 pm*, aber bei Zügen und Flügen benutzt man *sixteen-thirty*.

❷ ◖⬭46 Here is part of the conversation. Put Anna's questions back into the text. Then listen again and check.

a Do you go home early?
b Do you have a hot meal?
c Do you take work home with you?
d Do you take a lunch break?
e Do you work at weekends?

Anna: …¹
Mary: No, not very often. I usually leave the office at 5.30 or 6.
Anna: That's a long day. …²
Mary: Yes, I do. About 30 minutes.
Anna: And do you leave the office? …³
Mary: No, I don't. I eat a sandwich at my desk.
Anna: So you don't take a real break.
Mary: No, I stay in the office and check emails.
Anna: You work very hard. …⁴
Mary: No, I don't. I never do that.
Anna: And what about Saturday and Sunday? …⁵
Mary: No, the weekend is free.
Anna: That's good. And what do you do?
Mary: Oh, Tim and I eat out or we go to a movie. We often go jogging together too. We exercise once or twice a week.

👥 **Now you. Ask and answer with a partner.**

❸ Use the table to write about your routines.

The days of the week
Monday
Tuesday
Wednesday
Thursday
Friday
Saturday
Sunday

KEY BUSINESS LANGUAGE

- on Monday(s)
- every day except Tuesdays
- at the weekend
- on Friday morning/afternoon/ evening
- in the morning/afternoon/ evening
- once/twice a day/week
- three/four/… times a day/week

I	always sometimes often usually never	get to check contact eat drink do leave work	overtime. sports after work. coffee after lunch. work before 8 am. emails in my lunch break. the office before 5 pm. clients at the weekend. lunch in the canteen.

Talking about free time

1 Tim is Mary's husband. Read about his week. Complete the text.

> do · go · like · enjoy listening · like watching · play · work

Hi, I'm Tim. I work part-time as a music producer. I ....¹ from home a lot and manage the house and the children. In my free time I ....² squash on Wednesdays, and I ....³ jogging twice a week, too. I sometimes ....⁴ yoga with Mary on Tuesdays. When Mary comes home from work, we ....⁵ TV together. We also ....⁶ to music. At the weekend we ....⁷ eating out or we do sports together.

🔊47 **Listen and check.**

2 Answer the questions.

	Yes, he does.	No, he doesn't.
1 Does Tim work full-time?	☐	☐
2 Does he go jogging two days a week?	☐	☐
3 Does he watch TV with Mary in the evenings?	☐	☐
4 Does he do sports with Mary?	☐	☐

3 Now you. Write about your hobbies. Use *go*, *play* or *do*.

I .... I .... I ....

4 What do you like doing? Tick the boxes.

Activities	You	Student 1	Student 2
doing sports	☐	☐	☐
going for walks	☐	☐	☐
being online	☐	☐	☐
reading	☐	☐	☐
listening to music	☐	☐	☐
eating out	☐	☐	☐
going to the cinema / theatre / concerts	☐	☐	☐

👥 **Now ask two other students. What do they like doing?**

Do you like doing sports?

No, I don't. I'm not very sporty. But I enjoy watching tennis on TV.

Do you like listening to music?

Sometimes, but I prefer reading books.

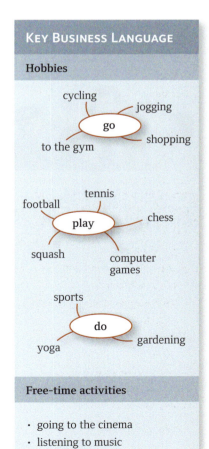

KEY BUSINESS LANGUAGE

Hobbies

cycling · jogging · **go** · to the gym · shopping

football · tennis · **play** · chess · squash · computer games

sports · **do** · yoga · gardening

Free-time activities
- going to the cinema
- listening to music
- reading
- watching TV

Simple Present Einfache Gegenwart

I/You	**work**	as an assistant.
He/She/It	**lives**	in Spain.
We/You/They	**finish**	work at 5.30.

Negative form	Verneinung	
I/You	**don't** work	for AOL.
He/She/It	**doesn't** work	in Munich.
We/You/They	**don't** work	together.

- Wir bilden verneinte Sätze mit **don't/doesn't**.
- I/you/we/they: **don't** he/she/it: **doesn't**
- Nach *doesn't* hängen wir kein **s** an das Verb an.

⟶ ❶❷

Questions Fragen

Do	I/you	**work**	part-time?
Does	he/she/it	**start**	early?
Do	we/you/they	**meet**	once a week?

- Wir bilden Fragen und Kurzantworten mit **do** und **does**.
- **Do** I/you/we/they …? **Does** he/she/it …?

⟶ ❸

Short answers Kurzantworten

Do you **work** at Blue Coast Electronics? – Yes, I **do**. / No I **don't**.

Does he **work** overtime? – Yes, he **does**. / No he **doesn't**.

Do they **finish** before six? – Yes, they **do**. / No, they **don't**.

⟶ ❸

I like showing visitors around.

Verb + -ing Verb + -ing

I **like** show**ing** visitors around.

We **love** talk**ing** about our free time.

He **hates** work**ing** overtime.

- Nach *love, like, hate, prefer* hängen wir **-ing** an das folgende Verb an.

⟶ ❹

Adverbs of frequency Adverbien der Häufigkeit

I	**usually**	have	tea at 4 pm.	
You	**normally**	check	your emails	**three times a day.**
Her boss	**rarely**	sends	emails.	
We	**often**	work	overtime.	
They		have	a meeting	**every day.**

- Wir stellen Adverbien aus einem Wort vor das Verb.
- Aber wir stellen sie hinter Formen von *be*: *Jack* **is usually** *in his offic*e.
- Andere Adverbien der Häufigkeit stehen am Ende (oder Anfang) des Satzes.

⟶ ❺

Notes

① **Read the sentences about people in this unit. Correct the wrong information.**

1 James Manning works in a supermarket.

  .He.doesn't.work.in.a.supermarket..He.works.in.a.sandwich.production.company.......

2 Mary Thompson eats lunch in the staff restaurant. ....

3 Mary and her husband go to the theatre at the weekend. ....

4 James Manning goes home at 6 in the morning. ....

5 James Manning and his girlfriend have lunch together. ....

② **Complete the email with positive or negative forms of the verbs in the box.**

check · do · have · leave · sleep · take · ~~work~~

… and some of my colleagues have a big problem with their work-life balance. They all .work.

very long hours. They ....¹ the office at 4 or 5 pm – most of them are there

until late in the evening. They all ....² problems with stress. They

........................³ a lunch break every day. They ....⁴ three or four hours a

night, and they ....⁵ sports. At the weekends they all ....⁶

their emails on their mobile phones.

③ **🔊48 Listen to a video clip from the website of Fashionista, a fashion-design company based in Mexico City. Answer the questions with short answers.**

1 Does Luis come from Mexico? ....

2 Does he live in Mexico City? ....

3 Are the company's headquarters in Spain? ....

4 Does the company have a factory in Venezuela? ....

5 Does the company make jeans? ....

6 Do people in Europe buy Fashionista's jeans? ....

④ **Write sentences about things you (don't) like. Use phrases from the box.**

1 .I.like.having.coffee.breaks.......... 4 .I.don't.like.starting.work.early......

2 .... 5 ....

3 .... 6 ....

· start work early
· work overtime
· get emails
· show visitors around
· work at the computer
· make photocopies
· call customers
· have English lessons

👥 Compare your sentences with a partner. Does he or she like the same activities?

⑤ **Is a or b the correct position for the adverb of frequency?**

1	Andreas	**a** works	**b** overtime.	sometimes
2	Mary and Luca	**a** are	**b** early.	always
3	My colleagues	**a** get	**b** to work before 9.	rarely
4	My department	**a** has	**b** a team meeting every Tuesday.	usually
5	We meet	**a** for coffee	**b** and have an informal meeting.	every day

1 Read your text, then answer your partner's questions. Use the table below.

Partner A has a text about Magoma Karenga, Partner B has a text about Bianca da Silva.

Magoma Karenga

Bianca da Silva

→ Partner A: page 64;   → Partner B: page 66

Where What time Why What	does	he/she	live? work? leave home? get to work? eat lunch? eat for lunch? finish work? get home? do in the evening?

2 What is your routine? Complete the table. Then ask a partner.

	Morning	Afternoon
Monday		
Tuesday		
Wednesday		
Thursday		
Friday		
Saturday		
Sunday		

What do you do on Monday morning?

I usually have a team meeting.

3 Work in pairs. Ask and answer the questions, then report to the class.

1 When do you get to work?

Before 7 am	Between 7 and 8 am	Between 8 and 9 am	After 9 am
☐	☐	☐	☐

2 Do you take a lunch break?

Always	Usually	Sometimes	Never
☐	☐	☐	☐

3 How often do you work overtime?

Every day	Once a week	Once a month	Never
☐	☐	☐	☐

4 How often do you exercise?

Every day	Twice a week	Once a week	Never
☐	☐	☐	☐

5 How long do you normally sleep?

5 hours	6 hours	7 hours	8 hours or more
☐	☐	☐	☐

6 Do you take work home at the weekend?

Always	Usually	Sometimes	Never
☐	☐	☐	☐

7 How often do you check your emails?

Once a day	Twice a day	Three times a day	Four or more times a day
☐	☐	☐	☐

4 Write sentences with *I like* and *I don't like*.

I like............................. I don't like.........................

....

Tell a partner. Then ask him/her.

Do you like ...?

What don't you like?

REAL WORLD

Find out what free-time activities the company Google offers its employees. Tell the class.

Reviews and reports

⋯⋯⋗ Learning objectives

You will learn how to:
- say dates
- talk about the past
- give a report
- write emails

Sie lernen:
- Daten anzugeben
- über Vergangenes zu reden
- Bericht zu erstatten
- E-Mails zu schreiben

Key language
- months
- ordinal numbers
- regular business events

- *was/wasn't, were/weren't*
- *started, didn't start*
- *had, didn't have*

❶ **Match the headlines to the newsletter excerpts. Which event does the photo show?**

A A Big Job   **B** A Great Night   **C** A New Product

D A New Policy   **E** A New Office

BLUE COAST
E L E C T R O N I C S

1 ☐ *On May 20th Blue Coast opened its first sales administration center in Mexico. …*
2 ☐ *Our T4 cell phone is a big hit in Europe. Sales for June, the first month, were 80,000. …*
3 ☐ *Blue Coast had its mid-summer party early this year. …*
4 ☐ *Blue Coast's new Chief Financial Officer started work at the beginning of July. …*
5 ☐ *For the first time this year staff can give feedback to their managers. …*

❷  **Ask and answer the following questions.**

1 Does your company have a staff newsletter?
2 Does your company have any new products at the moment?
3 Does your company organize parties for staff?
4 Are there any new managers in your company?

The year
1960 *nineteen sixty*
2010 *twenty ten*
      two thousand (and) ten

The date
9/11/1989

Say (on) November (the) ninth,
     nineteen eighty-nine
     (on) the ninth of November,
     nineteen eighty-nine

Write *November 9, 1989*
       9 November 1989

In North America you write the month first: 11/09/1989.

Months and dates

January	July
February	August
March	September
April	October
May	November
June	December

1st first	13th thirteenth
2nd second	14th fourteenth
3rd third	15th fifteenth
4th fourth	16th sixteenth
5th fifth	17th seventeenth
6th sixth	18th eighteenth
7th seventh	19th nineteenth
8th eighth	20th twentieth
9th ninth	21st twenty first
10th tenth	…
11th eleventh	30th thirtieth
12th twelfth	31st thirty-first

on Monday, Tuesday, …

in
— spring
— summer
— autumn 🇬🇧 / fall 🇺🇸
— winter

Was it a good year?

1 Complete the sentences with words from the box.

Monday · Friday · today · tomorrow · week · ~~yesterday~~ · year

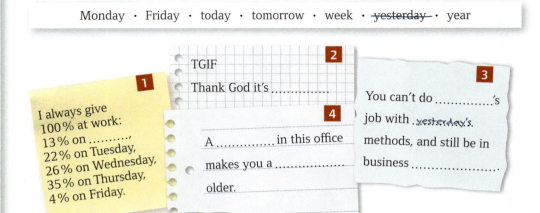

1 I always give 100% at work: 13% on ………, 22% on Tuesday, 26% on Wednesday, 35% on Thursday, 4% on Friday.

2 TGIF Thank God it's …………

4 A …………… in this office makes you a ……………… older.

3 You can't do …………'s job with *yesterday's* methods, and still be in business ………………

2 Match the dates and the events.

1 ☐ 15 September 2008   a the first day of the euro
2 ☐ 1 January 2002   b Lehman Brothers went bankrupt
3 ☐ November 9, 1989   c the launch of IBM's first personal computer
4 ☐ August 12, 1981   d the fall of the Berlin Wall

🔊49 **Listen and repeat the dates.**

3 🔊50 **Listen and tick the correct number.**

a ☐ 1st / ☐ 3rd   c ☐ 24th / ☐ 25th   e ☐ 4th / ☐ 14th
b ☐ 16th / ☐ 6th   d ☐ 30th / ☐ 13th   f ☐ 15th / ☐ 5th

4 🔊51 **Listen and write down the date in each dialogue.**

1 ....   3 ....
2 ....   4 ....

5 👥 **Complete the 'you' part of this table, then ask a partner.**

	You	A partner
My birthday is on		
My last holiday was in		
My last English lesson was on		
My first day in my company was		
My last performance review was on/in		
My last meeting was on		
My next meeting is on		

👥 **Now tell a different partner one of your dates. He/She must identify it.**

The sixteenth of June.

Is that your birthday?

Yes it is.

6 **Read the articles from two companies' end-of-year reviews, then do the task.**

1 Last June Blue Coast started its new 360° feedback system. First the managers gave feedback to the people in their department. But then there was something new. The department staff answered questions about their manager. One manager in the sales department said: "I was nervous about this idea but now I like it. People were very positive about my performance, but they were unhappy about some things in the department. I can now change those things."

Peggy Wu, HR manager

Peggy Wu, Blue Coast Electronics

2 Last May we had a big order for our new 256 GB memory cards from an important client in the United Arab Emirates. We had just three months for this order. Our production people in Oakland worked overtime in June, July and August. Normally they go on vacation in the summer, but this year it wasn't possible. So thanks to everyone in our production department. You did a great job.

Mario Rossi, Head of Production

Mario Rossi, Blue Coast Electronics

3 Last year was a difficult year for Capital City. An external report about our financial services in Asia was very negative, and the shareholders at the AGM in June weren't happy with the situation. So in September we restructured our operations in Asia. We also have a new CFO, Mark Carrington. He knows the Asian market very well.

Jane Hunter, Corporate Communications

4 Last year Capital City organized a special training workshop for all its HR managers. We stayed in a hotel in Brighton for three days – from 3 to 5 October – and discussed new ideas about staff training and staff motivation. There were also presentations from top HR consultants from the US. "It was very interesting," said Lara Thorpe, an HR manager in the London head office.

Ian Bartlett, Head of HR

Jane Hunter, Capital City

Ian Bartlett, Capital City

Match these sentences to texts 1–4.

a ☐ A new manager started work.
b ☐ A new product was a big success.
c ☐ Managers were happy about an event.
d ☐ A manager was nervous about a new system.

7 **Match the questions and answers.**

1 ☐ Were the sales people happy with the new system?
2 ☐ Was the order from the Arab world large?
3 ☐ Were shareholders happy with the company's performance?
4 ☐ Was Lara one of the consultants?

a Yes, it was.
b No, they weren't.
c No, she wasn't.
d Yes, they were.

8 **Complete the sentences with the verbs in the box.**

discussed · restructured · stayed · started · was · wasn't · were · worked

1 Blue Coast .... its new feedback system in June.
2 The people in the sales department .... unhappy about some things.
3 The deadline for the order .... a problem.
4 The production staff .... overtime.
5 Last year .... a great year for Capital City.
6 Capital City .... its Asian operations.
7 The HR managers .... in a hotel in Brighton.
8 They .... new ideas for staff motivation and training.

KEY BUSINESS LANGUAGE

shareholder
consultant
client
people
CEO (Chief Executive Officer)
CFO (Chief Financial Officer)
manager

deadline
AGM (Annual General Meeting)
staff party
events
workshop
performance review

Giving a report

1 🔊52 **Brian Smith is a consultant at Capital City Financial Services. He visited a company called Fashion Plus last week. Listen to Brian's report and tick true or false.**

		true	false
1	Fashion Plus didn't have a good year last year.	☐	☐
2	It closed 24 shops in France, Germany and the UK.	☐	☐
3	It moved production to Asia six months ago.	☐	☐
4	Brian visited a Fashion Plus shop.	☐	☐

2 **Complete Jane Malone's report about the visit to Fashion Plus.**

discussed · had · stopped

REPORT ON VISIT TO FASHION PLUS IN SOUTHAMPTON – Friday, 14 February

My first meeting of the day was with the Head of Design. She started in the company a year ago and made a lot of changes in the first six months. She ....[1] old product lines and focussed on young fashion for young people. The product portfolio this year is attractive, fresh and stylish.

Then I saw three managers from the sales and marketing department. We had a very interesting discussion. Last year they changed the marketing strategy of the company. Now they are very happy with the situation, but there are some problems with the sales figures in ten shops in the north of England.

In the afternoon I ....[2] a telephone conference with the Head of Logistics and the Head of Production. We ....[3] production schedules and delivery deadlines. They were very well informed. After my telephone conference I decided to check the company's sales figures. I didn't have a lot of time so I didn't join the video conference discussion.

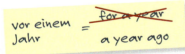

vor einem Jahr = ~~for a year~~ a year ago

3 👥 **Use some of the sentence beginnings below to make notes about your last meeting. Give a short report to the rest of the group.**

· Last week / month / Two months ago / In May I had a meeting with …
· The meeting was in …
· It was about …
· It started at … and finished at …
· First, we discussed …
· There was a presentation about …
· Mr/Ms X gave a report about …
· Later / After the presentation / After the report we discussed …
· We had a telephone/video conference with …
· At the end of the meeting we decided to …
· The meeting was / wasn't a success because …

Writing emails

1 **Read this email from Mr Sutherland's PA (Personal Assistant), Mariella, to Brian Smith. What does Mr Sutherland want Brian to do?**

asap   *as soon as possible*
(say the letters *a s a p* and not
asap in one word.)

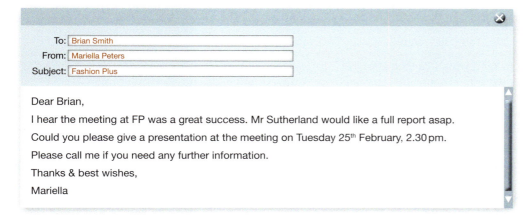

To: Brian Smith
From: Mariella Peters
Subject: Fashion Plus

Dear Brian,

I hear the meeting at FP was a great success. Mr Sutherland would like a full report asap.

Could you please give a presentation at the meeting on Tuesday 25th February, 2.30 pm.

Please call me if you need any further information.

Thanks & best wishes,

Mariella

2 **Brian writes to Rose Jackson at Fashion Plus. Complete the email.**

Best · Could you please · Dear · I would like to · Please call me · Thank you

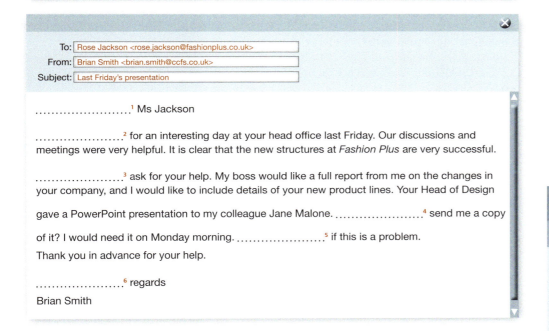

To: Rose Jackson <rose.jackson@fashionplus.co.uk>
From: Brian Smith <brian.smith@ccfs.co.uk>
Subject: Last Friday's presentation

........................¹ Ms Jackson

........................² for an interesting day at your head office last Friday. Our discussions and meetings were very helpful. It is clear that the new structures at *Fashion Plus* are very successful.

........................³ ask for your help. My boss would like a full report from me on the changes in your company, and I would like to include details of your new product lines. Your Head of Design gave a PowerPoint presentation to my colleague Jane Malone. ....⁴ send me a copy of it? I would need it on Monday morning. ....⁵ if this is a problem.
Thank you in advance for your help.

........................⁶ regards
Brian Smith

3 **Rose Jackson replies to Brian Smith's email. Put the sentences in the correct order.**

To: Brian Smith <brian.smith@ccfs.co.uk>
From: Rose Jackson <rose.jackson@fashionplus.co.uk>
Subject: Re: Last Friday's presentation

☐ I am very pleased that you were happy with your visit here last Friday.
☐ Thank you for your email of Thursday 20 February.
☐ Please find attached the PowerPoint presentation about the new product lines in our company.
☐ Kind regards
1 Dear Mr Smith
5 I hope your presentation goes well.

KEY BUSINESS LANGUAGE

Writing emails

· Dear … *(formal/neutral)*
· Hello … *(formal/neutral)*
· Hi … *(informal)*

· Thank you for …
· Could you please send me …?
· Please find attached …

· Please call me if
 … you need any further information.
 … you have (any) questions.
 … this is a problem.
· Thank you in advance.

· Kind/Best regards
· Best wishes

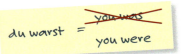

du warst = ~~you was~~
you were

Was/Were – Simple past of *to be*   *Was/Were – einfache Vergangenheit von to be*

Positive	Negative
I **was**	I **wasn't**
You **were**	You **weren't**
He/She/It **was**	He/She/It **wasn't**
We/You/They **were**	We/You/They **weren't**

*Richard **was** in London last week.*
*I **wasn't** in London for the conference. We **were** in Berlin.*

⋯⟶ **1 3**

Questions with *was/were*   *Fragen mit was/were*

Was I …?	Yes, I **was**. / No, I **wasn't**.
Were you …?	Yes, you **were**. / No, you **weren't**.
Was he/she/it …?	Yes, he/she/it **was**. / No, he/she/it **wasn't**.
Were we/you/they …?	Yes, we/you/they **were**. / No, we/you/they **weren't**.
When were you there? **Where was** he?	I **was** there in 2011 He **was** in Frankfurt.

***Was** the staff party good? – Yes, it **was**.*
***Where was** the staff party last year? – It **was** in Oakland.*

⋯⟶ **2**

Simple past of regular verbs   *Einfache Vergangenheit regelmäßiger Verben*

I/You/He/She/It	**worked** last Saturday.
We/You/They	**worked** last Saturday.

Negative form

I/You/He/She/It	**didn't work** last Sunday.
We/You/They	**didn't work** last Sunday.

- Wir hängen **-(e)d** an das Verb.
- **work – work**ed, **decide – decid**ed.
- Wir bilden die Verneinung mit **didn't** (= **did not**) + Infinitiv.

⋯⟶ **3**

Simple past of irregular verbs   *Einfache Vergangenheit unregelmäßiger Verben*

Present	Past
give	**gave**
have/has	**had**
make	**made**
say	**said**
see	**saw**

- Unregelmäßige Verben haben eigene Formen.
- Die Verneinung wird mit **didn't** + Infinitiv gebildet – wie bei regelmäßigen Verben.

*I **gave** my boss the report yesterday.*
*We **made** a lot of money last year.*
*I **didn't have** a good day yesterday.*
*Ann **didn't see** Max at the meeting.*

⋯⟶ **4**

How was your trip to Paris?

Great! I saw my hotel and the conference room.

1 Fill in *was(n't)* and *were(n't)*.

Sandra has two children. Yesterday the children ....¹ at a birthday party. The party ....² in the afternoon. Sandra ....³ in the office at that time. She had a meeting with her boss. The meeting ....⁴ very long and Sandra ....⁵ (not) happy. There ....⁶ many things to discuss. The meeting finished at 7 pm. Sandra ....⁷ tired. She ....⁸ back home at 8 pm. The children still had a lot of energy. They ....⁹ (not) tired!

2 👥 Write down questions with *was* or *were*. Then ask and answer them.

1 How many colleagues / at the last office party? ....

2 there / any mistakes / in your last report? ....

3 you in the office / on Monday? ....

4 your last meeting / a success? ....

3 Read about Colin's week.

Colin: Hello, Jill. How are you? I had a wonderful week. Things were great. On Monday I had a good performance review. So I gave a party in the evening. On Thursday morning I had a very good meeting with my boss. It was a great week.

Jill's week was stressful. Complete the text. Use negative forms.

Jill: Hello, Colin. Well, my week wasn't very good. Things were difficult.

I .... have a good performance review on Monday. So I ....
....
....

4 John Carpenter works for Capital City. Complete his report with the verbs in the simple past.

Report on visit to Auto Quick – 12 March

CAPITAL CITY
FINANCIAL SERVICES

On Monday 12 April I ....¹ (visit) Auto Quick, a car wash company in Birmingham.

We ....² (start) the day with a tour of an Auto Quick car wash centre in the city.

Then the Head of Marketing ....³ (give) a presentation about the company.

After that I ....⁴ (discuss) the company's performance with the management. The

company ....⁵ (have) a good year last year. It ....⁶ (open)

four new car wash centres in the UK. I ....⁷ (see and talk) to people in all the

departments. It ....⁸ (be) a very good day.

1 Fill in dates on your timeline.

	school	first job	this job	last holiday

from _____ to _____ | _____ | _____ | _____

👥 **Tell a partner about your life.**

2 Jane Malone was away last week. Write Brian Smith's questions.

1 you / were / where / last week / ?

....

2 you / how long / away / were / ?

....

3 and / so long / why / ?

....

4 a / visit / was / success / the / ?

....

5 problem / was / the / what?

....

3 🔊 53 **Listen to the conversation between Jane and Brian. Write answers to the questions in 2 .**

1 ....

2 ....

3 ....

4 ....

5 ....

4 What is true for you? Tick the boxes.

	yes	no
(have) a birthday party last year	☐	☐
(have) a performance review last year	☐	☐
(have) a good holiday last year	☐	☐
(visit) another country last month	☐	☐
(have) a good day yesterday	☐	☐
(give) a presentation last week	☐	☐
(make) coffee yesterday	☐	☐
(see) a good film last week	☐	☐
(work) last weekend	☐	☐

👥 **Tell a partner what you did and what you didn't do.**

5 How was your performance last year? Choose 1, 2, 3, 4 or 5.

MY PERFORMANCE LAST YEAR

1 = never, 3 = sometimes, 5 = always

I was on time for meetings.	1	2	3	4	5
I worked well with my colleagues.	1	2	3	4	5
I answered my emails quickly.	1	2	3	4	5
I enjoyed my work.	1	2	3	4	5
The company's clients were happy with my performance.	1	2	3	4	5

👥 **Now talk to a partner. Were there any problems last year?**

6 You are John Carpenter (see page 53, task 4). Write an email to Ken Underwood, the CFO of **Auto Quick**.

- Thank him for the successful meeting on Monday, 12 March.
- Send an attachment – report on the meeting.
- Ask him for the sales figures for the first quarter of this year asap.
- End the email.

To: ....
From: john.carpenter@ccfs.co.uk
Re: Sales figures

....
....
....
....
....
....
....

REAL WORLD

Look at some real emails in English. If you don't have any, ask your colleagues if they can help. Write down any useful phrases you find.

Business travel

1 **What do people say when they meet at an airport? Match the parts.**

1 Welcome to London. I'm Brian Smith.

2 Is this your first visit here?

a That's very kind of you, but I'm OK.

b It was fine, thank you.

d No, thanks. I had something on the plane.

c Pleased to meet you, Brian.

4 Can I help you with your bag?

3 How was your flight?

5 Would you like something to eat or drink?

e Yes, it is.

54 **Now listen and check.**

2 55 **Jane Malone meets Carla Rossi at the airport. Listen and answer the questions.**

1 How late is Carla?
☐ Three hours. ☐ Four hours. ☐ Five hours.

2 Why is she late?
☐ The weather in Rome was bad.
☐ The plane had a technical problem.
☐ There was a strike.

You will learn how to:
· talk about journeys
· talk about agendas
· give directions
· order in a restaurant
· make small talk

Sie lernen:
· über Reisen zu erzählen
· Tagesordnungen besprechen
· Wegbeschreibungen zu geben
· im Restaurant zu bestellen
· wie man Smalltalk macht

Key language:
· business travel terms
· directions
· restaurant phrases

· Simple past questions and short answers

Travel problems

❶ **Karolin Bauer from Blue Coast's Munich office flew to London yesterday for a meeting at Capital City's headquarters. Put her story in the correct order.**

Correct order: 1 *e*   3 ☐   5 ☐   7 ☐

2 *g*   4 ☐   6 ☐   8 ☐

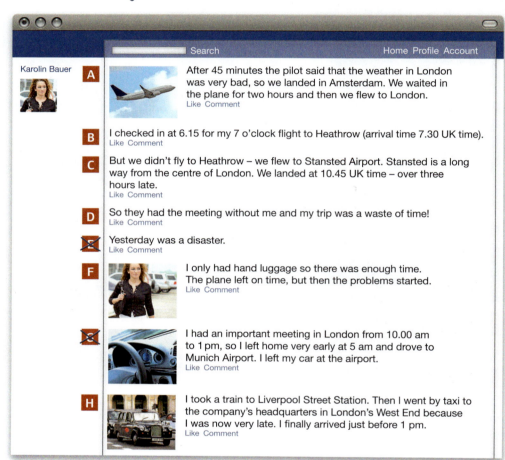

Karolin Bauer

A After 45 minutes the pilot said that the weather in London was very bad, so we landed in Amsterdam. We waited in the plane for two hours and then we flew to London.
Like Comment

B I checked in at 6.15 for my 7 o'clock flight to Heathrow (arrival time 7.30 UK time).
Like Comment

C But we didn't fly to Heathrow – we flew to Stansted Airport. Stansted is a long way from the centre of London. We landed at 10.45 UK time – over three hours late.
Like Comment

D So they had the meeting without me and my trip was a waste of time!
Like Comment

E Yesterday was a disaster.
Like Comment

F I only had hand luggage so there was enough time. The plane left on time, but then the problems started.
Like Comment

G I had an important meeting in London from 10.00 am to 1 pm, so I left home very early at 5 am and drove to Munich Airport. I left my car at the airport.
Like Comment

H I took a train to Liverpool Street Station. Then I went by taxi to the company's headquarters in London's West End because I was now very late. I finally arrived just before 1 pm.
Like Comment

◉ 56 **Now listen and check.**

❷ **How did Karolin get there? Find one answer from each box for each part of the journey.**

By train.   In a taxi.
By plane.   By car.

How did she get ...
1 ... from home to Munich Airport?
2 ... from Germany to England?
3 ... from Stansted to the centre of London?
4 ... from Liverpool Street Station to Capital City's offices?

She drove.   She flew.
She went on the train.
She took a cab.

❸ 👥 **Talk about travel.**

| How do you travel | ... when you go on holiday? |
| | ... when you go away on business? |

| How do you get | ... to work? |
| | ... to the shops? |

I drive.
I walk.
I go by ...

> **You can always say:**
> go by + (means of transport)
> go by car
> go by train
> go by bus
>
> *zu Fuß gehen* = walk

Questions about a meeting

1 Look at the agenda for the meeting at Capital City. Match the sentences on the right to the correct item on the agenda.

CAPITAL CITY
FINANCIAL SERVICES

AGENDA

Meeting in Conference Room 604 on 16 April, 10.00 – 13.00.

Participants	William Green (WG)
	Brian Smith (BS)
	Jane Malone (JM)
	Mark Richardson (MR), CFO, Blue Coast, San Francisco
	Conor Griffin (CG), Project Specialist, Blue Coast, Munich
	Karolin Bauer (KB), Head of Business Development, Blue Coast, Munich

Item 1   **Introductions**

Item 2   **MINUTES OF LAST MEETING** (JM)

Item 3   **Changes at Blue coast**
New offices (MR)

Item 4   **Blue Coast's quarterly results**
Report on results for Q1 (MR)

Item 5   **Plans for new products**
Report on new mobile phones and tablet PCs (CG)

Item 6   **Sales targets in Europe**
Report on this year's sales targets for mobile phones and tablet PCs (KB)

Item 7   **Capital City's investment**
Investment plans this year (BS)

Item 8   **AOB (Any other business)**

c We plan to sell 5 % more phones and tablet PCs this year.

a We plan to put the T5 phone on the market in October this year.

d OK. If there are no more points, we can finish and go to lunch.

e Last year we opened a new sales centre in Monterrey, Mexico.

b We can invest €15 million in your European operations.

h My name's Jane Malone. I'm a consultant here at Capital City.

f The participants agreed to meet in London on 16th April.

g Our January to March sales figures in Asia and Europe were good.

2 Karolin Bauer arrived at the end of the meeting, so she asked her colleague Conor Griffin for a report. Complete her questions.

1 Did you get my text …
2 When did you …
3 Did Capital City have anything to …
4 Did they like our new product …
5 Did Ursel send the sales …
6 Did Capital City make …

a … say about our US results?
b … message?
c … targets for Europe?
d … designs?
e … an investment decision?
f … start?

3 🔊57 Match Conor Griffin's answers to Karolin's questions in **2**. Then listen and check.

a Yes, they did. We can have €15 million for our European operations.
b Yes, they did. They really liked our new T5.
c Yes, I did. How frustrating for you!
d Yes, she did. She mailed all the sales documentation.
e At 10. We didn't wait because your report was item 6 on the agenda.
f No, they didn't. But they were very happy with our figures for Europe and Asia.

KEY BUSINESS LANGUAGE

introduction   discussion point
AOB
plan   result
agenda
minutes   action point
summary   target

Giving directions

1 **Which way? Match the symbols with the expressions from the box.**

a go back
b go to the end
c turn left
d ~~go straight on~~
e turn right
f go past

1 ☐
2 ☐
3 ☐

4 ☐
5 *d*
6 ☐

2 **Look at the map. Where's the … ?**

1 ☐ bank
2 ☐ hotel
3 ☐ bookshop

a on Miller Road
b in the High Street opposite the pharmacy
c 100 m up King Street on the right

3 🔊 58 **After the meeting at Capital City, Karolin wants to meet an old friend for a meal. Karolin phones her. Listen and decide: is the restaurant 1, 2, 3 or 4 on the map?**

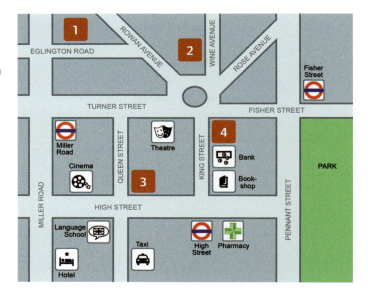

4 **Give directions from the cinema to the Fisher Street underground station.**

> the pharmacy on the right · at the next corner ·
> opposite the park on the right · along the High Street

1 Go straight ....

2 Go past ....

3 Turn left ....

4 Fisher Street Underground station is ....

👥 **Give a partner directions from the Happy Hour bistro to the Miller Road Underground station.**

5 👥 **Give a partner directions. Use the map in exercise 3 .**

➡ *Partner A: page 64;*   ➡ *Partner B: page 66*

In the restaurant

1 **Complete the dialogue in the restaurant with the sentences from the box.**

> A glass of red wine for me, please. · The carrot and ginger soup, please, and then the
> quiche and salad. · We have a reservation in the name of Tomkins.

Waiter: Good evening. How many is it for? Two?

Sonia: Yes. ………………………………………

Waiter: Tomkins. Oh yes. The table over here next to the window.
So here's the menu for you. Today's specials are on the board.

Sonia: Thanks.

Waiter: Would you like something to drink?

Sonia: ……………………………………… The Spanish rioja.

Karolin: And I'd like a gin and tonic.

Waiter: A glass of rioja, and a gin and tonic. Sure. I'll be right back.

Waiter: Here you are. A glass of rioja and a gin and tonic.

Sonia: Thanks.

Waiter: Are you ready to order now?

Sonia: Karolin?

Karolin: ………………………………………

Waiter: OK.

Sonia: And I'd like the salad to start and the chicken curry for my main course.

👥 🔊59 **Listen and check. Then read the dialogue with two partners.**

2 **Make sentences.**

1 Weber / in the name of / a reservation / I have ……………………………………………

2 please / mineral water, / We'd like / a large bottle / of ……………………………………………

3 ready / order / to / We're ……………………………………………

4 to start and / the melon / I'd like / as my main course / the fish ……………………………………………

5 again, / the menu / please / we / Could / have ……………………………………………

3 🔊60 **Put the parts of the dialogue in order. Then listen and check.**

a **Karolin:** Very nice. We went to Syria.   1 ▢   2 ▢   3 ▢
    Sonia: Syria. That's unusual.
    Karolin: Yes, but it's a great country.
    Sonia: Interesting.

b **Sonia:** Fine thanks. We had a trip to Prague last weekend.
    Karolin: Prague. That's nice. Was it good?
    Sonia: Great. How was your last holiday?

c **Karolin:** … and they had the meeting without me. But my
    colleague was there and he gave me an update.
    Sonia: OK. So how is the job? Do you still like it?
    Karolin: It's alright.
    How's Julian?

👥 **Practise the dialogue, then ask a partner: How was your last holiday?**

KEY BUSINESS LANGUAGE

At the restaurant

- I have a reservation in the name of …
- Could we have … please?
- I'd like a …
- I'm/We're ready to order.
- I'd like the … to start and the … for/as my main course.
- Excuse me.
- Yes, please. / No, thank you.

Yesterday I left the car next to the warehouse.

More irregular verbs   Weitere unregelmäßige Verben

Present	Past	Present	Past	Present	Past
buy	bought	drink	drank	fly	flew
come	came	eat	ate	get	got
cost	cost	fall	fell	give	gave
do	did	feel	felt	go	went
drive	drove	find	found	hear	heard

Present	Past	Present	Past	Present	Past
know	knew	put	put	send	sent
leave	left	read	read	speak	spoke
make	made	say	said	take	took
meet	met	see	saw	tell	told
pay	paid	sell	sold	think	thought

· *read* wird in der Vergangenheit /red/ ausgesprochen.

→ ❶❷

Questions and short answers in the simple past
Fragen und Kurzantworten in der einfachen Vergangenheit

Where	did	you	have	your meeting?	
When	did	she	arrive?		
Why	did	they	work	last weekend?	
How	did	he	get	to the restaurant?	
	Did	she	have	a good trip?	Yes, she **did**. / No, she **didn't**.
	Did	you	eat	at the hotel?	Yes, we **did**. / No, we **didn't**.
	Did	he	give	a presentation?	Yes, he **did**. / No, he **didn't**.

· Wir bilden Fragen in der einfachen Vergangenheit mit **did**.
· **did** wird in der Kurzantwort wiederholt.

→ ❸

1 Write in the missing forms.

Present	Simple past	Negative simple past
arrive	1	2 ....
fly	3	4 ....
5	went	6 ....
leave	7	8 ....
9	10	didn't say
see	11	12 ....
take	13	14 ....

2 Fill in the simple past forms. Use the verbs in the brackets.

Last week my colleague Susanna ....[1] (go) to an international conference in Rome. She ....[2] (fly) from Berlin to Rome. She ....[3] (have) breakfast at 5.00 am! At 5.30 she ....[4] (take) a taxi to the airport. She ....[5] (check in) and then she ....[6] (read) a magazine. At 7 she ....[7] (look at) the monitor. The plane ....[8] (be) late! Susanna ....[9] (call) her office and ....[10] (write) some emails. The plane ....[11] (leave) at 9.45! Susanna ....[12] (not/arrive) on time.

3 Before she went to Rome, Susanna gave her assistant a list of tasks. Complete the dialogue.

– book a room for the sales meeting next week ✗
– call our supplier in Mannheim about the new price list ✔
– drive the car back to Hertz ✔
– translate the minutes of the last sales meeting into Italian ✗

Susanna: Did ....[1]?

Lynn: Yes, I did. They emailed the new price list yesterday.

Susanna: ....[2] for the sales meeting this week?

Lynn: Oh, I'm sorry, I had no time.

Susanna: No problem. ....[3] the car back to Hertz?

Lynn: ....[4] I drove it back two hours ago.

Susanna: ....[5] the minutes of the last sales meeting?

Lynn: ....[6] I couldn't find them.

1 Complete this story in a business magazine.

> didn't hear · flew · gave · had · landed ·
> made · thought · took · was · went

Last month I ....¹ a stressful trip to the US. I
..................² from London Heathrow to New York (JFK).
It was a comfortable flight and the plane ....³ on
time at 3.30 pm US time. I ....⁴ through passport
control and got my bag. Then I ....⁵ a taxi to my
hotel in Manhattan. I had a dinner appointment with a
client in a restaurant in Chinatown at 7.00 pm. It was about
5.15 then and I ....⁶ a very bad mistake. I went
to bed. You see, for me it was 10.15 pm UK time. I
..................⁷ tired so I ....⁸: "45 minutes sleep,
then a quick shower and a taxi to Wong Hu's restaurant".
The problem was that I ....⁹ my alarm. But I was
lucky. I contacted my client the next morning. He was OK
about the problem and ....¹⁰ me a large order.

2 👥 Ask a partner about a meeting. Make questions with
the words below.

> ~~have~~
> read   discuss
>   meet
> know   write
> take   drink
>
> minutes   notes
> a formal agenda   coffee
>   all the people there
> visitors
>   plans

Did you have a formal agenda? ....
....
....
....

3 👥 Look at the map. Write directions, then ask and
answer.

Partner A: ▬ ～ ▬
From the café to the police station:
First, you ....

Partner B: ▬ ～ ▬
From the restaurant to the language school:
First, you ....

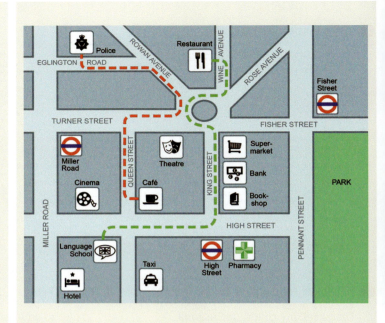

4 👥 What is your favourite restaurant? Where is it?
Give a partner directions to the restaurant.

5 You are in your favourite restaurant. What's on the
menu?

Starters	*Main courses*	*Dessert*
....	....	....
....	....	....
....	....	....

👥 One of you is the waiter and two of you are
customers. Order food and drink.

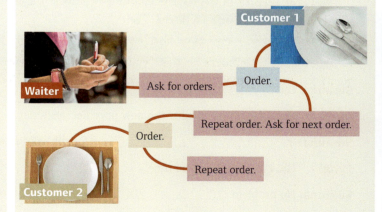

REAL WORLD

Look at an online English menu. What would you like to eat?
Tell your class in the next lesson.

Partner A

Complete these questions. Then ask your partner and write down the answers. ➜ *Unit 2, page 16, Task 4*

1 Where's Bob? ....

2 Where .... Mira? ....

3 Where .... Tim and Michael? ....

4 .... Susan? ....

Now answer your partner's questions. Use this information.

Lily	on vacation
Sam and Martin	in a meeting
Peter	at lunch
Tina	on a business trip

The phone rings. Answer it. Your boss is not there. Take a message for her. Das Telefon ➜ *Unit 2, page 19, Task 7*
klingelt. Melden Sie sich. Ihre Chefin ist nicht da. Schreiben Sie eine kurze Nachricht für sie.

Information
Your name: David Miles
Your company: TPT Engineers
Your boss's name: Louise Hastings (She is on a business trip today.)

Call

Message for: ....

From: ....

Company: ....

Message: ....

There are three differences between your picture and your partner's picture. Ask ➜ *Unit 3, page 27, Task 7*
questions and answer your partner's questions to find the differences.
Es gibt drei Unterschiede zwischen Ihrem Bild und dem Bild, das Ihr Partner / Ihre Partnerin
hat. Stellen Sie Fragen und beantworten Sie die Fragen Ihres Partners / Ihrer Partnerin, um die
Unterschiede herauszufinden.

Is there a …?

Yes, there is. /
No, there isn't.

Is the flip chart in the
corner / at the front /
next to the window?

It's at the front.

The three differences are:

1 ....
....

2 ....
....

3 ....
....

→ *Unit 4, page 35, Task 8*

Ask your partner about his/her company. Write the information in the table below.

Name:	....
Name of company:	....
Department:	....
Products:	....
Offices in the USA:	....

Here is some information about you and your company. Answer your partner's questions.

Name: Alex Winter
Name of company: Windpower Ltd.
Department: Production
Products: windmills, turbines
Offices in the UK: Three (Bristol, Liverpool and Cardiff)

Check your information with your partner.

→ *Unit 5, page 46, Task 1*

Read your text about Magoma Karenga, then answer your partner's questions.

Magoma Karenga

I ride a taxi bicycle (our word for a taxi bicycle is boda boda) in Kampala in Uganda. I don't live in Kampala. I live in a small village near the city with my wife and three children. I leave home early at 6.30 in the morning and ride my boda boda into the city centre. My work starts at 8 o'clock. I work from 8 to 1 pm. I have a long lunch break from 1 to 3.30 – it's very hot at lunchtime. Usually I sit with colleagues in the park. We eat pawpaw or banana and drink water. Then I work until 6 pm. I get home at 7.30 and eat with my family. I often watch TV after dinner. I work 5 days a week and sometimes I work 6 days. My job is hard so I always go to bed at 9 or 9.30.

Ask your partner questions about Bianca da Silva. Use the table on page 46.

→ *Unit 7, page 58, Task 5*

Tell your partner to start at Fisher Street underground station. Give him/her directions to the hotel, but don't mention the destination. Then ask your partner where he/she is.

Your partner gives you directions. At the end tell him/her where you are.

Partner B

Answer your partner's questions. Use this information.

→ Unit 2, page 16, Task 4

Bob	on vacation
Mira	ill
Tim and Michael	on a training course
Susan	at lunch

Now complete these questions. Then ask your partner and write down the answers.

1   Where's Lily?   ....

2   Where .... Sam and Martin?   ....

3   .... Peter?   ....

4   .... Tina?   ....

You call TPT Engineers. You would like to speak to Louise Hastings. If she is not there, leave a message.   Sie rufen TPT Engineers an und möchten Louise Hastings sprechen. Hinterlassen Sie eine Nachricht, falls sie nicht da ist.

→ Unit 2, page 19, Task 7

Information

Your name:	Thilo Krause
Your company:	OZG Transport Hamburg
Phone number:	0049 40 312 7548
Message:	Please call back. It's about brochures.

There are three differences between your picture and your partner's picture. Ask questions and answer your partner's questions to find the differences.
Es gibt drei Unterschiede zwischen Ihrem Bild und dem Bild, das Ihr Partner / Ihre Partnerin hat. Stellen Sie Fragen und beantworten Sie die Fragen Ihres Partners / Ihrer Partnerin, um die Unterschiede herauszufinden.

→ Unit 3, page 27, Task 7

Yes, there is. / No, there isn't.

Is there a …?

Is the flip chart in the corner / at the front / next to the window?

It's at the front.

Where are the loudspeakers?

Are there any chairs/ documents/…?

They are on the wall at the back/on the left/…

Yes, there are. / No, there aren't. There are two/three/…

The three differences are:

1 ....

....

2 ....

....

3 ....

....

→ Unit 4, page 35, Task 8

Here is some information about you and your company. Answer your partner's questions.

Name:	Charlie Miles
Name of company:	Games Box Inc.
Department:	Design
Products:	Computer games, games apps for mobile phones
Offices in the USA:	Two (Seattle and Chicago)

Interview your partner. Write the information in the table below.

Name:	....
Name of company:	....
Department:	....
Products:	....
Offices in the UK:	....

Check your information with your partner.

→ Unit 5, page 46, Task 1

Ask your partner questions about Magoma Karenga. Use the table on page 46.
Read your text about Bianca da Silva, then answer your partner's questions.

Bianca da Silva

I work in São Paulo in a fashion design company. My company is in the centre of the city, but my apartment isn't in the centre. I leave home at 7.30 in the morning and go by bus to the centre of São Paulo. São Paulo sometimes has transport problems. On good days I get to work at 8.30, on bad days I get to work late at 9 o' clock or 9.30! I have a normal work routine with lunch at 12.30. I don't go out into the city centre at lunchtime. It's very hot. There is air conditioning in the office, so I have a sandwich there. I finish work at 5 pm and I get home at 6.30. In the evening I often meet friends in a café or go to the cinema.

→ Unit 7, page 58, Task 5

Your partner gives you directions. At the end tell him / her where you are.

Tell your partner to start at the pharmacy. Give him / her directions to the theatre, but don't mention the destination. Then ask your partner where he / she is.

Unit 1 - Welcome

🔊 02   Page 8, Exercise 1

1   My name's Maria Santos.
2   I'm an administrative assistant.
3   I'm a project manager with Blue Coast.
4   It's an electronics company.

🔊 03   Page 8, Exercise 3

Maria: Good morning. Blue Coast Electronics. How can I help you?
Jan: Hello Melanie. This is Jan Wagner. I'm a project manager in the Munich office.
Maria: Sorry, this is Maria not Melanie. Maria Santos. I'm the administrative assistant here in the design department.
Jan: Oh sorry, Maria. Is Melanie Kim in the office? She's the new software designer.
Maria: Just a moment, please. Here's Melanie.
Jan: Thank you, Maria.
Maria: You're welcome, Jan.
Melanie, it's Jan Wagner from Munich for you.

🔊 04   Page 9, Exercise 4

Melanie: Hello. Melanie Kim speaking.
Jan: Hello, Melanie. This is Jan Wagner in the Munich office. How are you?
Melanie: Fine, thanks. And you?
Jan: Fine, thank you. So, today is your first day! Welcome to Blue Coast!
Melanie: Thanks, Jan. What's your job in the Munich office?
Jan: I'm a project manager in R & D. You know, the research and development department.
And you are a software designer, right?
Melanie: That's right.

🔊 05   Page 9, Exercise 5

1   Good morning.   Good morning.
2   Thank you!   You're welcome!
3   What's your job?   I'm an assistant.
4   Where are your   In the USA.
    headquarters?
5   Mark Smith speaking.   Hello. This is Kristin Miller.
6   How are you?   Fine, thanks. And you?

🔊 06   Page 10, Exercise 1

This is Jan Wagner.
He's with Blue Coast Electronics in Munich.
He's a project manager in the research and development department.

This is Melanie Kim.
She's with Blue Coast Electronics in San Francisco.
She's a software designer in the design department.

🔊 07   Page 10, Exercise 2

Adam: Hello. My name's Adam Brown. I'm a production manager here in San Francisco. And what's your name?
Conor: I'm Conor Griffin.
Adam: So, what's your job at Blue Coast?
Conor: I'm a project specialist in the research and development department.
Adam: Where are you based?
Conor: I'm based in Munich.

🔊 08   Page 11, Exercise 4

Maria: Hi Peter. How are you?
Peter: Not bad, thanks. And you?
Maria: Fine. Peter, this is Melanie Kim, our new software designer. Melanie, this is Peter. He's in the production department.
Melanie: Hi Peter. So, what's your job?
Peter: I'm an administrative assistant.
Maria: Peter's from New York.
Peter: Where are you from, Melanie?
Melanie: I'm from Florida.

🔊 09   Page 14, Exercise 4

Maria: Good morning, Blue Coast Electronics. Maria Santos speaking. How can I help you?
David: Hello. This is David Pennant from IT Austria in Vienna. Is Melanie Kim in the office today?
Maria: Just a moment, please.
Melanie: Melanie Kim.
David: Hello, Ms Kim. This is David Pennant from IT Austria in Vienna.
Melanie: Hello, Mr Pennant. How are you?
David: I'm fine, thanks. So, you are the new software designer in Blue Coast's San Francisco office.
Melanie: That's right.

Unit 2 – At work

🔊 10   Page 15, Exercise 3

Gail: Good morning, Blue Coast Electronics. Gail Anderson speaking. How can I help you?
Jan: Good morning. This is Jan Wagner. Is Sandra Li in the office, please?
Gail: I'm sorry. She's on a training course today. Can I help you?
Jan: Yes, can Sandra please …

🔊 11 Page 16, Exercise 1

1	Where's Anne today?	She's on vacation.
2	Where is Eric?	He's on a training course.
3	Where is Martin?	He's on a business trip.
4	Where are Bill and Ellen?	Bill and Ellen are at lunch.
5	Where are Jane and Peter?	They're in a meeting.
6	Where is Rebecca?	She's off sick.

🔊 12 Page 16, Exercise 3

Call 1

Gail: Good morning, Blue Coast Electronics. Gail Anderson speaking. How can I help you?

Ken: Hello. My name's Ken Upton. Is Kim Becker, the design assistant, in the office today?

Gail: I'm sorry. She's on a training course. Can I take a message?

Call 2

Gail: Good morning, Blue Coast Electronics. Gail Anderson speaking. How can I help you?

Amanda: Good morning. This is Amanda Cooke. Is José Perez, the project manager, in the office today?

Gail: I'm sorry. He's off sick.

Amanda: Is the project assistant there?

Gail: Yes, she is. Just a moment, please.

Call 3

Gail: Good afternoon, Blue Coast Electronics. Gail Anderson speaking. How can I help you?

Steven: Good afternoon. This is Steven Delgado. Can I speak to Amanda Ford, the design engineer, please?

Gail: I'm sorry. She's on a business trip today. Can I take a message?

🔊 13 Page 17, Exercise 1

Gail: Good afternoon. Blue Coast Electronics. Logistics department. Gail speaking.

Ralf: Good afternoon. This is Ralf Hillman. Can I speak to Jessica Marks, please?

Gail: I'm sorry. She's on the telephone at the moment. Can I take a message?

Ralf: Yes, please. Can she call me back?

Gail: Of course. What's your phone number, please?

Ralf: I'm in Berlin. The country code is 49, the area code is 30, and the number is 471 00 26. That's my direct line.

Gail: OK. Thank you for your call, Mr Hillman.

Ralf: You're welcome. Goodbye.

Gail: Goodbye.

🔊 14 Page 17, Exercise 2

zero	two	four	six	eight
one	three	five	seven	nine

🔊 15 Page 17, Exercise 3

a	12 345 67	**c**	88 03 432
b	559 34 78	**d**	1-312-667-4000

🔊 16 Page 17, Exercise 5

a b c d e f g h i j k l m n o p q r s t u v w x y z

🔊 17 Page 18, Exercise 1

Gail: Good afternoon. This is Gail speaking.

James: Good afternoon. This is James Watson from Humber and Webber in the UK. Can I speak to Martin Springer, please?

Gail: I'm sorry. He's not in at the moment. He's on a business trip.

James: Oh. Can he call me back?

Gail: Of course. Your name is James ...

James: Watson.

Gail: James Watson. And the company is ...

James: Humber and Webber.

Gail: Sorry, this is not a good line. Can you repeat that for me, please?

James: Sure. Humber H-U-M-B-E-R and Webber W-E-B-B-E-R.

Gail: OK, I have that now. And the number is ...

James: Country code 44.

Gail: So, 0044.

James: And the area code is 1392.

Gail: 1392.

James: And the number is 225162.

Gail: 225162. OK, I've got that, Mr Watson. Thank you for your call.

James: Have a nice day.

Gail: You too. Goodbye.

🔊 18 Page 18, Exercise 2

1 **A:** Can I speak to Ellen, please?
  B: I'm sorry. She's not in at the moment.
  A: Can she call me back?
  B: Of course. Can you give me your number?

2 **A:** Thank you for your call.
  B: You're welcome. Have a nice day
  A: Thank you. You too.

3 **A:** Can she call me back?
  B: Of course. Can you give me your number, please?
  A: I'm in Ireland. The country code is 353 and the number is 1 2894981.
  B: OK. Fine.

4 **A:** Good morning, Wendy Baxter speaking.
  B: Is this the production department?
  A: Yes, it is. How can I help you?
  B: Can I speak to Eric Reed, please?

🔊19 Page 19, Exercise 4 + 5

Sandra: Good morning. Keynote Systems, this is Sandra West speaking. How can I help you?

Conor: Good morning, Ms West. This is Conor Griffin from Blue Coast Electronics in Munich. Can I speak to Andrew White, please?

Sandra: I'm sorry, Mr Griffin. He can't come to the phone at the moment. Can I take a message?

Conor: Yes, please. Can he send me the new brochures?

Sandra: Of course. Can you spell your name, please?

Conor: Certainly, it's C-O-N-O-R G-R-I-F-F-I-N.

Sandra: OK, I have that. And can you give me your address, please?

Conor: Of course, it's Bergweg 7, 81241 Pasing in Germany.

Sandra: I'm sorry, I can't speak German, so can you spell the name of the street and the town, please?

Conor: Yes, it's Bergweg, that's B-E-R-G-W-E-G, number 7, in Pasing, that's P-A-S-I-N-G.

Sandra: OK. Can I check that, please? It's Mr Conor Griffin, and the address is Bergweg, that's B-E-R-G-W-E-G, number 7, 81241 Pasing, that's P-A-S-I-N-G, in Germany.

Conor: Yes, that's right.

Sandra: OK, thanks. Have a nice day.

Conor: Thank you. You too. Goodbye.

Sandra: You're welcome. Goodbye.

🔊20 Page 19, Exercise 6

Sandra: Good morning. Keynote Systems. Sandra West speaking. How can I help you?

Markus: Good morning. This is Markus Schmidt from ADW Systems in Munich. Can I speak to Kim Turner, please?

Sandra: I'm sorry, Mr Schmidt. She can't come to the phone at the moment. Can I take a message?

Markus: Yes, please. Can she call me back? It's about her business trip next week.

Sandra: Of course. Can you repeat the name of the company, please?

Markus: Yes, it's ADW Systems. That's A-D-W.

Sandra: OK, thank you. Can you give me your number, please?

Markus: Yes, it's country code 0049, then 89 523 4106.

Sandra: I'm sorry. That's 0049 89 …

Markus: Yes, 0049 89 523 4106

Sandra: Thank you. Can I repeat your details? You're Markus Schmidt from ADW Systems and your number is 0049 89 523 4106.

Markus: Yes, that's right.

Sandra: Thank you for calling, Mr Schmidt. Goodbye.

Markus: Goodbye.

🔊21 Page 22, Exercise 2

1 **A:** Can you give me the order number, please?
  B: Yes, it's 9981 JJE.
2 **A:** Can you give me the order number, please?
  B: Yes, it's JZW 698 VIVA.
3 **A:** Can you give me the order number, please?
  B: Yes, it's UZG 733 TC.
4 **A:** Can you give me the order number, please?
  B: Yes, it's T45DD NAKG.

🔊22 Page 22, Exercise 3

Julia: Good morning. PCB Electronics, Julia Redman speaking. How can I help you?

James: Good morning. This is James Gray from Keynote Systems in Lausanne.
Can I speak to Jürgen Stenglein, please?

Julia: I'm sorry, Mr Gray. He's at lunch at the moment. Can I take a message?

James: Yes, please. Can he call me back? It's about my order.

Julia: Of course. Can you give me the order number, please?

James: Yes, it's UFG 733 TC.

Julia: Oh, can I check that, please? UFG 733 TC?

James: That's right.

Julia: OK. Thank you for your call, Mr Gray.

🔊23 Page 22, Exercise 4

Roger: Good morning. XMP Software Systems. Roger Sands speaking. How can I help you?

Carla: Hello. This is Carla Lopez. Is David Hu there?

Roger: I'm sorry. He's on a business trip. Can I take a message?

Carla: Yes, please. It's about our new website. Can he call me back?

Roger: Certainly, Ms Lopez. Can I have your phone number, please?

Carla: It's 001 (for the USA), 858 (for San Diego), then 742 8155.

Roger: That's 001 858 742 8155. And what's the name of your company, please?

Carla: PTEC. That's P-T-E-C.

Roger: OK. Thank you for calling, Ms Lopez. Goodbye.

Unit 3 – Around the company

🔊24 Page 23, Exercise 2

1	plant	5	desk	9	mobile phone
2	monitor	6	book	10	chair
3	computer	7	mouse	11	coffee machine
4	water cooler	8	photocopier	12	window

🔊25 **Page 24, Exercise 1**

Jessica: Excuse me. Are you Jan Wagner?
Jan: That's right.
Jessica: I'm Jessica Marks. Nice to meet you.
Jan: Nice to meet you too.
Jessica: Welcome to California.
Jan: Thank you.
Jessica: Can I take your coat?
Jan: Thank you. Here you are.

🔊26 **Page 24, Exercise 3**

Jessica: Jan, can I introduce you to Martina Williams? Martina is in the logistics department. Martina, this is Jan Wagner from our Munich office.
Jan: Nice to meet you, Ms Williams.
Martina: Nice to meet you too. Please call me Martina.

🔊27 **Page 25, Exercise 1**

Jessica: Can I show you around?
Jan: Yes please. Head office is so big. Our Munich office is small.
Jessica: Well, we have a production department here at headquarters. Look, here's the floor plan. We're here in reception. And this is the production area, this yellow area over here on the left.

🔊28 **Page 25, Exercise 2**

Jessica: So that is reception and the production area, and these are the other departments.
Jan: Right.
Jessica: The reception area is blue of course – we're Blue Coast – and it's next to administration, that's this pink area here. And that's next to the logistics department.
Jan: That's your department.
Jessica: Yes, that's right, I'm in logistics. And then there are four other office departments – these other four pink areas on the plan. There's also a warehouse, here.

🔊29 **Page 25, Exercise 3**

Jan: Can you show me the conference room, please?
Jessica: Yes, of course. The conference room for your presentation. It's the green area on the floor plan. This way, please.
Jan: And can you tell me where the toilets are?
Jessica: The restrooms? Sure. They're along here – on the right.

🔊30 **Page 25, Exercise 4**

Dan: Welcome to Micro Supplies, Carla. I'm Dan Whitman, Head of Sales.
Carla: Pleased to meet you, Dan.
Dan: Can I give you a tour?

Carla: Thank you.
Dan: So, we're here in the reception area. This way, please. OK, well here on the right next to the HR department is the logistics department.
Carla: And your department?
Dan: The sales department is here on the left, between the finance department and the purchasing department.
Carla: I see. So is that where our meeting is?
Dan: No, our meeting is in the conference room here on the right, directly opposite the finance department. Look!
Carla: Mm. It's perfect for presentations and meetings.
Dan: It is. Right, well here we are at the end of the corridor. The administration area is here on the left. And that's Micro Supplies.
Carla: Er, Dan. And where are the restrooms?
Dan: Oh yes, they're here on the right, next to the administration area.
Carla: Thanks, Dan.
Dan: You're welcome.

🔊31 **Page 26, Exercise 1**

Jan: Well, Jessica, this is my first visit to head office. It's very interesting. But … what's that? Can I hear children?
Jessica: Yes, you can. There's a childcare center here.
Jan: A childcare center? Wow!
Jessica: Yes, this is a great place to work. There's a shop for the staff. And a staff restaurant.
Jan: Ah! There's a staff restaurant in Munich. Er … a small staff restaurant.
Jessica: And there's a fitness studio here and a room for aerobics. Are there any sports facilities in the Munich office?
Jan: No, there aren't. It's a very small office. But there's a water cooler.
Jessica: A water cooler!
Jan: Yes, it's in reception.
Jessica: And the staff?
Jan: The staff? Oh! There aren't any water coolers in our offices. But … there's a staff car park.
Jessica: Really! There isn't a staff parking lot here in Frisco. There's a city parking lot opposite our head office. But it costs two dollars a day.
Jan: Ah!

🔊32 **Page 26, Exercise 3**

Jessica: So, Jan. Here's our visitor's office.
Jan: Very nice.
Jessica: Yes. You have a computer with high-speed internet on the desk, and the printer is here on this small table in front of the desk. There's extra paper for the printer in the corner on the left.
Jan: OK.
Jessica: There are power points under the desk here.

Jan: Ah yes. Good.

Jessica: OK, then on the wall behind the desk is the control panel for the air-conditioning.

Jan: Great.

Jessica: I think that's all.

Jan: What's that document on the desk next to the phone?

Jessica: Oh, that's the head office list – it has all the phone numbers and email addresses.

🔊33 **Page 27, Exercise 6**

Jessica: So, here's the conference room, Jan. I think it's perfect for your presentation. As you can see, the conference table has ten chairs. And there's a laptop and a pointer for presentations.

Jan: Great. And where's the projector?

Jessica: It's on the ceiling.

Jan: Ah! I see.

Jessica: There are blinds at the windows. And there is a whiteboard on the wall opposite the windows.

Jan: OK.

Jessica: And there are ten power points for laptops in the middle of the table.

Jan: Oh yes. That's very good. Er … I can't see loud-speakers.

Jessica: There are mini-loudspeakers here at the side.

Jan: Of course. Sorry. Can we have a video conference here?

Jessica: Certainly. The technology is installed. The microphones are here in the middle of the table, next to the power points. So, is everything OK?

Jan: Yes, thank you.

🔊34 **Page 30, Exercise 4**

Receptionist: Hello, you're Natalia Varsovia, is that right?

Natalia: Yes, I'm here for the company tour.

Receptionist: Well, here is a floor plan. We're here in the reception area. It's blue on the plan.

Natalia: OK. I see.

Receptionist: Here are the meeting rooms. They're on the left. They're yellow on the plan. They're next to the finance department. That's red on the plan.

Natalia: Thank you, I see. And where is the sales department?

Receptionist: The sales department is here, in front of you. On the plan it's this purple part on the left.

Natalia: Thanks. Where is the restroom, please?

Receptionist: The restroom? Yes, of course. There's one near here, between the purchasing depart-ment and the production area and ware-house. There's also one next to the recep-tion, on the left. They're brown on the plan.

Natalia: Thank you. Just a moment. …

Natalia: Thank you. So, can you show me the human resources department?

Receptionist: Yes, of course. The human resources department is here on the left, between the research and development department and the logistics department. It's green on the plan. So, this is the end of the tour. Do you have any questions?

Natalia: Thank you very much. I have one question. Where can I relax for a moment?

Receptionist: You can go to the garden. It's in the middle of the plan.

Natalia: Thank you very much.

Receptionist: You're welcome, Ms Varsovia.

Unit 4 – Colleagues and companies

🔊35 **Page 32, Exercise 1**

1 Woman: Gregory, this is Jan Wagner. He's a colleague from Germany. Jan, this is Gregory Swan. Gregory works in the finance department with me.

Gregory: Nice to meet you, Jan.

Jan: Nice to meet you too, Gregory.

2 Amina: Hello. I'm Amina Abbad.

Gregory: I'm Gregory Swan. Where are you from, Amina?

Amina: I'm from the Netherlands. I'm Dutch.

Woman: Amina is one of our European suppliers.

3 Woman: Can I introduce you to Stephan Camenzind? Stephan, this is Gregory.

Gregory: Nice to meet you.

Stephan: Nice to meet you too.

Woman: Stephan is one of our big European customers.

🔊36 **Page 32, Exercise 2**

1 Frank Lewis is Canadian. He has a company in Mon-treal. He buys cell phones from Blue Coast. He's a good customer. Blue Coast does a lot of business with him.

2 Isobel Lennox is British, she's from Scotland. She works for Hightime Electronics in Aberdeen.The company makes office equipment. Hightime Electronics sells to Blue Coast, but also to companies in Europe.

3 Yen Lee is one of Blue Coast's Chinese contacts. His company, RMT Electronics, has three factories in China. The company produces electronic components for Blue Coast. It supplies all Blue Coast's cell phone components. The people at Blue Coast say that Yen Lee's company does a very good job.

🔊 37 **Page 33, Exercise 1**

Claire: Hello, I'm Claire Gerber from Specialist Office Equipment in Zurich.

Isobel: Nice to meet you. I'm Isobel Lennox from Hightime Electronics. What does your company do?

Claire: We produce office equipment. Here's my card. I'm a hardware specialist in the purchasing department of our company.

Isobel: That's interesting. I work in the hardware department of my company. We supply office equipment too. We specialize in video conference equipment.

Claire: Really? We need a new supplier. Can I call you for more information?

Isobel: Of course. No problem. Here's my card.

Claire: That's great. Thanks very much.

Isobel: But I have a new email address. It's now lennox underscore isobel at hightime dot co dot uk.

🔊 38 **Page 33, Exercise 3**

Call 1

Melanie: Can I have your email address?

Supplier A: Sure. It's mike dot foster at opf dot com.

Melanie: Is that opf or ops?

Supplier A: It's opf.

Melanie: So, that's mike dot foster at opf dot com.

Supplier A: That's right.

Call 2

Supplier B: Can I give you our website address?

Melanie: Of course.

Supplier B: It's www dot pc hyphen systems dot co dot uk.

Melanie: Is that S-Y-S-T-E-M-S?

Supplier B: That's right.

Melanie: So, that's www dot pc hyphen systems dot co dot uk.

Supplier B: Correct.

Call 3

Supplier C: My email address is: jane underscore kent at akku dot at.

Melanie: Is that J-A-Y-N-E or J-A-N-E?

Supplier C: It's J-A-N-E.

Melanie: And the surname is Kent – K-E-N-T.

Supplier C: That's right.

Melanie: And can you spell the domain name?

Supplier C: Certainly. akku – that's A-K-K-U dot at.

Melanie: A-K-K-U dot at. Got it. Thank you.

Call 4

Supplier D: And our website address is: www dot cpu hyphen net dot com.

Melanie: Was that C-D-U?

Supplier D: No, C-P-U.

Melanie: I see. cpu hyphen net dot com.

Supplier D: That's right.

🔊 39 **Page 35, Exercise 5**

Good morning and welcome to our headquarters. Let me introduce myself. My name is Juliana Freitag. I'm the Sales Manager here at Bautechnik. We are a large company. We have our headquarters here in Ulm and offices in Hamburg, Frankfurt and Leipzig. But we are also a global company with offices in other parts of Europe, North America, India, China, Brazil, Turkey and Russia. We have …

🔊 40 **Page 35, Exercise 6**

1 **Speaker A:** What does your factory in the Netherlands produce?

  Juliana: It makes windows and doors for the European market.

2 **Speaker C:** How many offices do you have in China?

  Juliana: We have two.

3 **Speaker D:** How many employees are there in the Hamburg office?

  Juliana: There are ten. It's a small office.

4 **Speaker E:** What does your supplier in Jakarta supply?

  Juliana: Wood. 20,000 cubic metres a year.

5 **Speaker F:** How many products does your company have on its website?

  Juliana: Over 2,000.

6 **Speaker G:** How many suppliers do you have in South America?

  Juliana: Three – no, four. We have a new supplier in Buenos Aires now.

🔊 41 **Page 38, Exercise 2**

1 My mobile number is 0122 8451237 and my email address is peter_fox@hightime.co.uk. That's p-e-t-e-r underscore f-o-x at h-i-g-h-t-i-m-e dot co-dot-u-k.

2 I'm new. I don't have a phone number. But my email address is m_h@soe.ch. That's m underscore h at s-o-e dot c-h.

3 My office number is 040 3510 9988. You can email me at info@rdd.de. That's i-n-f-o at r-d-d dot d-e.

4 You can call me on 555 78526 or email me at andreas-wagner@intratech.at. That's a-n-d-r- e-a-s hyphen w-a-g-n-e-r at i-n-t-r-a-t-e-c-h dot a-t.

Unit 5 – Work schedules

🔊 42 **Page 39, Exercise 3**

Speaker 1: I work in a small company and there isn't a canteen. Normally I buy a sandwich in the bread shop opposite the company. There are some tables and chairs, so I eat my sandwich there and read the newspaper.

Speaker 2: There's a very good staff restaurant in our company. I eat a hot lunch there and talk to my colleagues.

Speaker 3: I work at home. At lunchtime I make a soup or some pasta in the microwave and listen to the radio.

Speaker 4: I work in sales. There is a staff restaurant in our company but it isn't near the sales department. Normally I eat a salad in my office and listen to hip-hop on my iPod.

🔊43 Page 40, Exercise 2

e **Speaker 1:** I start work early, at seven or half past seven.

Speaker 2: Really? I don't start before nine!

f **Speaker 1:** I switch on my computer and check my emails. That's the first thing.

Speaker 2: That's my first thing too.

a **Speaker 1:** At quarter past nine my colleagues and I usually have breakfast together.

Speaker 2: I don't have a breakfast break.

c **Speaker 1:** I often have lunch in the canteen.

Speaker 2: I don't like our canteen. I usually have lunch at my desk.

b **Speaker 1:** Before I go home, I check my emails one last time. I get between 30 and 40 emails a day.

Speaker 2: That's a lot. I get about 15 a day.

g **Speaker 1:** It's usually about quarter to four when I switch off my computer and leave.

Speaker 2: That's early, but you start early of course. I don't finish before five thirty or six.

d **Speaker 1:** But I sometimes work overtime. I don't like doing it.

Speaker 2: I can't do overtime, I have a family at home.

🔊44 Page 40, Exercise 3

eleven	sixteen	twenty-one	sixty
twelve	seventeen	twenty-two	seventy
thirteen	eighteen	thirty	eighty
fourteen	nineteen	forty	ninety
fifteen	twenty	fifty	a hundred

🔊45 Page 40, Exercise 4

a	15	**c**	30	**e**	55	**g**	77
b	20	**d**	45	**f**	66	**h**	89

🔊46 Page 42, Exercise 1+2

Anna: So how's your job, Mary?

Mary: Good, but there's a lot of stress.

Anna: Oh, why's that? What time do you start work?

Mary: 7.30.

Anna: 7.30? Do you always start so early?

Mary: Yes, I do. We're usually very busy in my department.

Anna: Do you go home early?

Mary: No, not very often. I usually leave the office at 5.30 or 6.

Anna: That's a long day. Do you take a lunch break?

Mary: Yes, I do. About 30 minutes.

Anna: And do you leave the office? Do you have a hot meal?

Mary: No, I don't. I eat a sandwich at my desk.

Anna: So you don't take a real break.

Mary: No, I stay in the office and check emails.

Anna: You work very hard. Do you take work home with you?

Mary: No, I don't. I never do that.

Anna: And what about Saturday and Sunday? Do you work at weekends?

Mary: No, the weekend is free.

Anna: That's good. So what do you do?

Mary: Oh, Tim and I eat out or we go to a movie. We often go jogging together too. We exercise once or twice a week.

🔊47 Page 43, Exercise 1

Tim: Hi, I'm Tim. I work part-time as a music producer. I work from home a lot, and manage the house and the children. In my free time I play squash on Wednesdays, and I go jogging twice a week too. I sometimes do yoga with Mary on Tuesdays. When Mary comes home from work we like watching TV together. We also enjoy listening to music. At the weekend we like eating out or we do sports together.

🔊48 Page 45, Exercise 3

Hi. Welcome to the Fashionista website. I'm Luis Escobar. I live and work in Mexico City but I don't come from Mexico. I come from Madrid in Spain. Fashionista's headquarters are here in Mexico City. We have 60 employees here in the city. We also have factories in Argentina and Chile. We make jeans for young people and we sell them here in Latin America, in Europe and in the United States.

Unit 6 – Reviews and reports

🔊49 Page 48, Exercise 2

1 the fifteenth of September two thousand and eight
2 the first of January two thousand and two
3 November ninth nineteen eighty-nine
4 August twelfth nineteen eighty-one

🔊50 Page 48, Exercise 3

a	the third	**c**	the twenty-fifth	**e**	the fourth
b	the sixteenth	**d**	the thirteenth	**f**	the fifth

🔊 51 Page 48, Exercise 4

1 **Speaker A:** When is my performance review this year?

Speaker B: It's on the twelfth of July.

2 **Speaker A:** When does the licence end?

Speaker B: It ends on the 31st of December two thousand and twenty-two.

3 **Speaker A:** So, Jake. You have a new job.

Speaker B: Yes. I start on September first.

4 **Speaker A:** When was the candidate born?

Speaker B: On March seventeenth 1979.

🔊 52 Page 50, Exercise 1

Good morning, everyone. Thank you for coming. As you know, Jane Malone and I had a meeting with the management of Fashion Plus in Southampton last Friday. The company didn't perform well last year. It had too many shops and its costs were high.

My day started with a presentation about the new structure of the company. Last year there were ten Fashion Plus shops in France and eight in Germany. But they weren't a success. So the company closed all these shops nine months ago. It also closed six shops here in the UK. The second problem last year was production costs. The old factory in the Czech Republic didn't have modern technology and the costs were too high. So six months ago Fashion Plus decided to move production to Morocco.

After the presentation, I had a meeting with the CFO and we discussed the new structure of the company. After lunch we visited a Fashion Plus shop in the city centre and talked to the staff there. At the end of the day we had a video conference discussion with the manager of the factory in Morocco. It was a very interesting day.

🔊 53 Page 54, Exercise 3

Brian: Hi, Jane. Where were you last week?

Jane: Oh, I was with a new client.

Brian: So how long were you away?

Jane: Three days. From Wednesday to Friday.

Brian: And why so long?

Jane: Well, the new client is in Aberdeen. That's 650 kilometres from London. So one day to get there, one day for the meetings in the company, and one day to travel back to London.

Brian: I see. Was the visit a success?

Jane: No, it wasn't. Well, not really.

Brian: Why? What was the problem?

Jane: The client didn't have all the company documentation.

Brian: I see.

Unit 7 – Business Travel

🔊 54 Page 55, Exercise 1

1 **Brian:** Welcome to London. I'm Brian Smith.

Visitor: Pleased to meet you, Brian.

2 **Brian:** Is this your first visit here?

Visitor: Yes, it is.

3 **Brian:** How was your flight?

Visitor: It was fine, thank you.

4 **Brian:** Can I help you with your bag?

Visitor: That's very kind of you, but I'm OK.

5 **Brian:** Would you like something to eat or drink?

Visitor: No, thanks. I had something on the plane.

🔊 55 Page 55, Exercise 2

Jane: Hello, Carla. Welcome to England. I'm Jane Malone.

Carla: Hello, Jane. I'm so sorry I'm late.

Jane: It's not a problem.

Carla: That's very kind of you. But four hours late!

Jane: Was the weather bad in Rome?

Carla: No, it wasn't. It was fine.

Jane: So what was the problem?

Carla: There was a small technical problem with the plane, so the airline put us on the next flight.

Jane: I see. Well, you're here now and that's fine.

🔊 56 Page 56, Exercise 1

Yesterday was a disaster. I had an important meeting in London from 10.00 am to 1 pm, so I left home very early at 5 am and drove to Munich Airport. I left my car at the airport.

I checked in at 6.15 for my seven o'clock flight to Heathrow (arrival time 7.30 UK time). I only had hand luggage so there was enough time. The plane left on time, but then the problems started.

After 45 minutes the pilot said that the weather in London was very bad, so we landed in Amsterdam. We waited in the plane for two hours and then we flew to London. But we didn't fly to Heathrow – we flew to Stansted Airport. Stansted is a long way from the centre of London. We landed at 10.45 UK time – over 3 hours late.

I took a train to Liverpool Street Station. Then I went by taxi to the company's headquarters in London's West End because I was now very late. I finally arrived just before 1 pm.

So they had the meeting without me and my trip was a waste of time!

Page 57, Exercise 3

Karolin: Conor, I'm so sorry. What a disaster! Did you get my text message?
Conor: Yes, I did. How frustrating for you!
Karolin: So, tell me. How was it? When did you start?
Conor: At 10. We didn't wait because your report was item 6 on the agenda – near the end of the meeting.
Karolin: I understand. What about item 4? Did Capital City have anything to say about our US results?
Conor: No, they didn't. But they were very happy with our figures for Europe and Asia.
Karolin: That's good. Did they like our new product designs?
Conor: Yes, they did. They really liked our new T5.
Karolin: Great! And item 6. Did Ursel send the sales targets for Europe?
Conor: Yes, she did. She mailed all the sales documentation.
Karolin: Thank goodness! And what about item 7? Did Capital City make an investment decision?
Conor: Yes, they did. We can have €15 million for our European operations.
Karolin: €15 million. Not bad. One more thing, Conor. May I have a copy of the minutes of the last meeting?
Conor: Certainly. I have a copy with me. But Karolin. Could we go to lunch now?
Karolin: Of course, Conor. Sorry. Where is lunch?
Conor: It's just along this corridor, on the right.

🔊 58 **Page 58, Exercise 3**

Sonia: So, Karolin: how was your meeting?
Karolin: I didn't have one.
Sonia: What?
Karolin: I had problems with my flight and arrived right at the end of the meeting.
Sonia: Oh no.
Karolin: Oh yes. I'll tell you all about it when we meet.
Sonia: OK.
Karolin: Can you give me directions to the restaurant?
Sonia: Sure. You're at the Maxwell Hotel on Miller Road, right?
Karolin: That's it.
Sonia: OK. Well, turn right when you come out of your hotel. Then turn right again into the High Street. Go straight on until you see the underground station on your right. Then turn left into King Street. It's not far.
Karolin: OK. Turn right out of my hotel, right again and then left into King Street.

Sonia: Yes, that's it. Then go to the end of King Street. When you come to the roundabout, cross over and go down Wine Avenue. The restaurant, well it's more a bistro, is called Happy Hour and it's about a hundred metres along on the left.
Karolin: OK, great. See you there.

🔊 59 **Page 59, Exercise 1**

Waiter: Good evening. How many is it for? Two?
Sonia: Yes. We have a reservation in the name of Tomkins.
Waiter: Tomkins. Oh yes. The table over here next to the window.
So here's the menu for you. Today's specials are on the board.
Sonia: Thanks.
Waiter: Would you like something to drink?
Sonia: A glass of red wine for me, please. The Spanish rioja.
Karolin: And I'd like a gin and tonic.
Waiter: A glass of rioja, and a gin and tonic. Sure. I'll be right back.
Waiter: Here you are. A glass of rioja and a gin and tonic.
Sonia: Thanks.
Waiter: Are you ready to order now?
Sonia: Karolin?
Karolin: The carrot and ginger soup, please, and then the quiche and salad.
Waiter: OK.
Sonia: And I'd like the salad to start and the chicken curry for my main course.

🔊 60 **Page 59, Exercise 3**

Karolin: ... and they had the meeting without me. But my colleague was there and he gave me an update.
Sonia: OK. So how is the job? Do you still like it?
Karolin: It's alright.
How's Julian?
Sonia: Fine thanks. We had a trip to Prague last weekend.
Karolin: Prague. That's nice. Was it good?
Sonia: Great. How was your last holiday?
Karolin: Very nice. We went to Syria.
Sonia: Syria. That's unusual.
Karolin: Yes, but it's a great country.
Sonia: Interesting.

Unit 1 - Welcome

Welcome

7 **unit** [ˈjuːnɪt] Einheit, Abteilung
welcome [ˈwelkəm] willkommen
to **look** [lʊk] ansehen, schauen
at [ət, æt] an, in, bei, auf, um, mit, zu, am, für

to **look at** [ˈlʊk ət] ansehen, betrachten
to **match** [mætʃ] zuordnen
the [ðə; ði] der, die, das, die (Plural)
photo [ˈfəʊtəʊ] Foto
word [wɜːd] Wort
to [tə,tu,tuː] in, mit, zu
people [ˈpiːpl] Leute, Menschen
are [ə, ɑː] bist, seid, sind
and [ənd, ən, ænd] und
thing [θɪŋ] Ding, Sache
laptop [ˈlæptɒp] Laptop
marker [ˈmɑːkə] Textmarker, Filzstift
to **flip** [flɪp] hin- und herspringen
flip chart [ˈflɪp tʃɑːt] Flip-Chart
manager [ˈmænɪdʒə] Geschäftsführer/in, Manager/in, Leiter/in

to **read** [riːd] lesen
to **do** [də,du,duː] tun, machen
list [lɪst] Liste
to-do list [təˈduː lɪst] Aufgabenliste
to **underline** [ˌʌndəˈlaɪn] unterstreichen
you [ju, juː] du, Sie, euch, man
to **understand** verstehen
[ˌʌndəˈstænd]
marketing [ˈmɑːkɪtɪŋ] Marketing, Vermarktung
to **meet** [miːt] (sich) treffen
meeting [ˈmiːtɪŋ] Besprechung, Sitzung, Treffen

marketing meeting Marketingbesprechung
[ˈmɑːkɪtɪŋ miːtɪŋ]
team [tiːm] Mannschaft, Team
to **send** [send] schicken, verschicken, abschicken

project [ˈprɒdʒekt] Projekt, Vorhaben, Arbeit
update [ˈʌpdeɪt] Aktualisierung, Update
project update Projektaktualisierung
[ˈprɒdʒekt ʌpdeɪt]
headquarters Hauptsitz, Zentrale
[ˈhedkwɔːtəz]
briefing [ˈbriːfɪŋ] Besprechung, Instruktion
with [wɪð,wɪθ] mit, bei
event [ɪˈvent] Veranstaltung
event manager [ɪˈvent Veranstaltungsmanager
mænɪdʒə]
from [frəm] von, aus, vor

Gourmet [ˈgʊəmeɪ] Feinschmecker-Restaurant
computer [kəmˈpjuːtə] Computer, Rechner
training [ˈtreɪnɪŋ] Ausbildung
computer training Computerkurs
[kəmˈpjuːtə treɪnɪŋ]
to **mail, e-mail, email** (per Post) schicken, mailen
[meɪl, ˈiːmeɪl]
website [ˈwebsaɪt] Website
text [tekst] Text, SMS
website text [ˈwebsaɪt Website-Text
tekst]
now [naʊ] jetzt, sofort, nun
what [wɒt] was, welche/r, was für ein
other [ˈʌðə] andere/r/s
English [ˈɪŋglɪʃ] englisch/e/r
to **know** [nəʊ] wissen, kennen
brainstorming Brainstorming, Ideen-
[ˈbreɪnstɔːmɪŋ] sammlung
Internet [ˈɪntənet] Internet
business [ˈbɪznəs] Geschäft, Firma
objective [əbˈdʒektɪv] Ziel
to **learn** [lɜːn] lernen
will [wɪl] werden
how [haʊ] wie
to **introduce** vorstellen
[ˌɪntrəˈdjuːs]
yourself [jɔːˈself] dich/sich, dich/sich (selbst)

the others [ði ˈʌðəz] die anderen
to **introduce oneself** sich vorstellen
[ɪntrəˌdjuːs wʌnˈself]
to **name** [neɪm] nennen
your [jɔː] dein/Ihr
job [dʒɒb] Stelle, Arbeitsplatz, Arbeit
company [ˈkʌmpəni] Firma, Gesellschaft
key [kiː] Schlüssel…
language [ˈlæŋgwɪdʒ] Sprache
key language [ˈkiː wichtige Redewendungen,
læŋgwɪdʒ] Schlüsselwörter
title [ˈtaɪtl] Titel
job title [ˈdʒɒb taɪtl] Berufsbezeichnung, Stellenbezeichnung

for [fə] für
telephone [ˈtelɪfəʊn] Telefon
call [kɔːl] Anruf, Gespräch
telephone call, phone Telefonanruf
call [ˈtelɪfəʊn kɔːl]
I [aɪ] ich
am [əm, æm] bin
not [nɒt] nicht
he [hi, hiː] er
she [ʃi, ʃiː] sie
it [ɪt] es

is [ɪz] — ist
we [wi] — wir
they [ðeɪ] — sie, man
a, an [ə; ən] — ein, eine
my [maɪ] — mein
his [hɪz] — sein
her [hə; hɜ:] — ihr
him [hɪm] — ihn, ihm
its [ɪts] — sein, ihr
our [ˈaʊə] — unser
their [ðeə] — ihr
name [neɪm] — Name
where [weə] — wo
What's your name? [ˌwɒts jɔ: ˈneɪm] — Wie heißen Sie?, Wie heißt du?
Where are you from? [weə ə ju ˈfrəm] — Woher kommen Sie?, Woher kommst du?
to be from … [bi ˈfrəm] — aus … kommen
based [beɪst] — einen Sitz haben, wohnen, niedergelassen sein

Skills – Hello

8 hello [həˈləʊ] — hallo
blue [blu:] — blau
coast [kəʊst] — Küste
electronics [ɪˌlekˈtrɒnɪks] — Elektronik
electronics company [ɪlekˌtrɒnɪks ˈkʌmpəni] — Elektronikhersteller
international [ˌɪntəˈnæʃnəl] — international, Auslands…
to listen [ˈlɪsn] — hören, zuhören
to connect [kəˈnekt] — verbinden, anschließen
sentence [ˈsentəns] — Satz
part [pɑ:t] — Teil
sentence part [ˈsentəns pɑ:t] — Satzteil
project manager [ˈprɒdʒekt mænɪdʒə] — Projektleiter/in, Auftragsleiter/in
administrative [ədˈmɪnɪstrətɪv] — Verwaltungs…
assistant [əˈsɪstənt] — Assistent/in
administrative assistant [ədˌmɪnɪstrətɪv əˈsɪstənt] — Verwaltungsassistent/in
card [kɑ:d] — Karte
business card [ˈbɪznəs kɑ:d] — Visitenkarte
design [dɪˈzaɪn] — Entwurf, Design, Gestaltung
here [hɪə] — hier, hierher, jetzt

department [dɪˈpɑ:tmənt] — Abteilung, Fachbereich
on the (tele)phone [ɒn ðə ˈtelɪfəʊn] — am Telefon
design department [dɪˈzaɪn dɪpɑ:tmənt] — Designabteilung
street [stri:t] — Straße
e-mail, email, mail [ˈi:meɪl, meɪl] — E-Mail
to complete [kəmˈpli:t] — beenden, ausfüllen, vervollständigen
profile [ˈprəʊfaɪl] — Profil, Beschreibung
site [saɪt] — Internetseite
networking site [ˈnetwɜ:kɪŋ saɪt] — soziales Netzwerk im Internet
network [ˈnetwɜ:k] — Netzwerk
to use [ju:z] — benutzen, verwenden, gebrauchen
information [ˌɪnfəˈmeɪʃn] — Informationen, Auskunft
in [ɪn] — in, bei, herein, da
worldwide [ˌwɜ:ldˈwaɪd] — weltweit
office [ˈɒfɪs] — Büro, Arbeitszimmer
skill [skɪl] — Geschick, Fähigkeit, Fertigkeit
office skills [ˈɒfɪs skɪls] — Fähigkeiten/Fertigkeiten für die Büroarbeit
worker [ˈwɜ:kə] — Arbeiter/in
office worker [ˈɒfɪs wɜ:kə] — Büroangestellte/r
who [hu:] — wer/wen/wem, der/die/das
good [gʊd] — gut
morning [ˈmɔ:nɪŋ] — Morgen, Vormittag
Good morning! [gʊd ˈmɔ:nɪŋ] — Guten Morgen!
can [kən, kæn] — können, dürfen
How can I help you? [haʊ kæn aɪ ˈhelp ju] — Wie kann ich dir/Ihnen/euch helfen?
this [ðɪs] — dies, das, diese/r/s hier
this is … (speaking) [ðɪs ɪs … ˈspi:kɪŋ] — am Telefon: Hier spricht …
Sorry. [ˈsɒri] — Tut mir leid., Entschuldigung.
software [ˈsɒftweə] — Software
new [nju:] — neu
designer [dɪˈzaɪnə] — Designer/in
software designer [ˈsɒftweə dɪzaɪnə] — Software-Entwickler/in
just [dʒʌst] — nur, wenig, etwas
moment [ˈməʊmənt] — Moment, Augenblick

Just a moment. [ˌdʒʌst ə ˈməʊmənt]	Einen Moment, bitte.	
Goodbye! [ˌɡʊdˈbaɪ]	Auf Wiedersehen!, Auf Wiederhören!	
Bye-bye! [baɪbaɪ]	Tschüss!	
please [pliːz]	bitte	
Thank you. [ˈθæŋk juː]	Danke.	
You're welcome. [jʊə ˈwelkəm]	Gern geschehen.	
dialogue [ˈdaɪəlɒɡ]	Dialog	
partner [ˈpaːtnə]	Partner/in	
on [ɒn]	auf, an	
evening [ˈiːvnɪŋ]	Abend	
afternoon [ˌaːftəˈnuːn]	Nachmittag	
phone [fəʊn]	Telefon	
Pleased to meet you. [pliːzd tə ˈmiːt ju]	Ich freue mich, Sie/dich/ euch kennen zu lernen.	

9
then [ðen]	dann
below [bɪˈləʊ]	unten, unter
to **check** [tʃek]	überprüfen, kontrollieren
to **speak** [spiːk]	sprechen, reden
How are you? [haʊ aː ˈju]	Wie geht es dir/Ihnen/ euch?
fine [faɪn]	gut, in Ordnung
thanks [θæŋks]	danke (umgangssprach- lich)
so [səʊ]	also
today [təˈdeɪ]	heute, heutzutage
first [fɜːst]	erste/r/s
day [deɪ]	Tag
research [rɪˈsɜːtʃ]	Forschung
development [dɪˈveləpmənt]	Entwicklung
that [ðæt]	das, der/die/das
right [raɪt]	richtig, rechts
That's right. [ˌðæts ˈraɪt]	Das stimmt.
best [best]	beste/r/s
reaction [riˈækʃn]	Reaktion
answer [ˈaːnsə]	Antwort, Lösung
to **ask** [aːsk]	fragen, bitten, auffordern
to **answer** [ˈaːnsə]	antworten, beantworten
question [ˈkwestʃən]	Frage
about [əˈbaʊt]	über
production [prəˈdʌkʃn]	Herstellung, Produktion
receptionist [rɪˈsepʃənɪst]	Empfangschef/in

Skills – Introductions

10
introduction [ˌɪntrəˈdʌkʃn]	Vorstellung, Einführung
production manager [prəˈdʌkʃn mænɪdʒə]	Produktionsleiter/in

specialist [ˈspeʃəlɪst]	Spezialist/in, Fachmann/ frau	
project specialist [ˈprɒdʒekt speʃəlɪst]	Projektspezialist/in, Experte/Expertin	
city [ˈsɪti]	Stadt, Großstadt	
which [wɪtʃ]	welche/r/s, der/die/das, was	
Which company are you with? [wɪtʃ ˈkʌmpəni aː ju wɪð]	Bei welcher Firma arbeitest du/arbeiten Sie/arbeitet ihr?	
leader [ˈliːdə]	Leiter/in, Vorsitzende/r	
project leader [ˈprɒdʒekt liːdə]	Projektleiter/in	
logistics [ləˈdʒɪstɪks]	Logisitk, Versorgung	

11
Hi! [haɪ]	Hallo!
conversation [ˌkɒnvəˈseɪʃn]	Gespräch, Unterhaltung
small [smɔːl]	klein
talk [tɔːk]	Gespräch, Gerede
small talk [ˈsmɔːl tɔːk]	Small Talk, Konversation
yes [jes]	ja, doch
I'm fine. [aɪm ˈfaɪn]	Mir geht's gut.

Grammar

12
grammar [ˈɡræmə]	Grammatik
verb [vɜːb]	Verb
to **be** [bi, biː]	sein
pronoun [ˈprəʊnaʊn]	Pronomen, Fürwort
short [ʃɔːt]	kurz, klein
form [fɔːm]	Form
short form [ʃɔːt ˈfɔːm]	Kurzform
spoken language [ˌspəʊkən ˈlæŋgwɪdʒ]	gesprochene Sprache
written language [ˌrɪtn ˈlæŋgwɪdʒ]	geschriebene Sprache, Schriftsprache
informal [ɪnˈfɔːml]	umgangssprachlich, nicht förmlich
positive [ˈpɒzətɪv]	positiv, bejahend
negative [ˈnegətɪv]	Verneinung, Negation
negative [ˈnegətɪv]	negativ, verneinend, verneint
or [ɔː]	oder
no [nəʊ]	nein
to **sound** [saʊnd]	klingen, sich anhören
unfriendly [ʌnˈfrendli]	unfreundlich
question word [ˈkwestʃən wɜːd]	Fragewort
personal pronoun [ˌpɜːsənl ˈprəʊnaʊn]	Personalpronomen
adjective [ˈædʒɪktɪv]	Adjektiv
to **express** [ɪkˈspres]	zum Ausdruck bringen, äußern, zeigen

possession [pəˈzeʃn]	Besitz
possessive determiner [pəˌzesɪv dɪˈtɜ:mɪnə]	besitzanzeigender Begleiter
genitive [ˈdʒenətɪv]	Genitiv

Grammar Practice

13	practice [ˈpræktɪs]	Übung
	grammar practice [ˈɡræmə præktɪs]	Grammatikübung
	to fill in [ˌfɪlˈɪn]	ausfüllen, eintragen
	of [əv]	von, aus
	two [tu:]	zwei
	colleague [ˈkɒli:ɡ]	Kollege, Kollegin
	research and development department [rɪˌsɜ:tʃ ənd dɪˌveləpmənt dɪˈpɑ:tmənt]	Forschungs- und Entwicklungsabteilung
	to correct [kəˈrekt]	verbessern, korrigieren
	these [ði:z]	diese, die (hier)
	statement [ˈsteɪtmənt]	Aussage, Erklärung
	to add [æd]	hinzufügen
	apostrophe [əˈpɒstrəfi]	Apostroph, Auslassungszeichen
	note [nəʊt]	Notiz, Nachricht, Anmerkung

Consolidation

14	consolidation [kənˈsɒlɪdeɪʃn]	Festigung
	to choose [tʃu:z]	wählen, aussuchen
	correct [kəˈrekt]	richtig, korrekt
	phrase [freɪz]	Satz
	telephone phrase [ˈtelɪfəʊn freɪz]	Redewendung für Gespräche am Telefon
	technology [tekˈnɒlədʒi]	Technologie
	IT =Information Technology [ˌaɪˈti:; ɪnfəˌmeɪʃn tekˈnɒlədʒi]	Informationstechnologie
	Mr [ˈmɪstə]	Herr
	to go [ɡəʊ]	gehen
	directory [dəˈrektəri]	Verzeichnis, Dateiverzeichnis
	to find [faɪnd]	finden, feststellen
	member [ˈmembə]	Mitglied
	to tell [tel]	erzählen, sagen
	class [klɑ:s]	Klasse, Kurs
	real [ˈri:əl]	echt
	world [wɜ:ld]	Welt
	Ms [mɪz]	Frau
	Xing [ksɪŋ]	Firmenname

Unit 2 – At work

At Work

15	to work [wɜ:k]	arbeiten, funktionieren
	work [wɜ:k]	Arbeit, Werk
	at work [ət ˈwɜ:k]	auf der Arbeit, im Büro
	picture [ˈpɪktʃə]	Bild
	place [pleɪs]	Ort, Stelle, Platz
	out [aʊt]	hinaus, heraus, nicht da, nicht zu Hause
	out of the office [aʊt əv ði: ˈɒfɪs]	nicht im Büro
	course [kɔ:s]	Kurs, Lehrgang
	training course [ˈtreɪnɪŋ kɔ:s]	Übungskurs
	to remember [rɪˈmembə]	sich erinnern an
	revision [rɪˈvɪʒn]	Korrektur, Überarbeitung, Änderung
	to take [teɪk]	nehmen
	message [ˈmesɪdʒ]	Nachricht
	to answer a call [ˌɑ:nsər ə ˈkɔ:l]	einen Anruf entgegennehmen
	to take a message [ˌteɪk ə ˈmesɪdʒ]	eine Nachricht entgegennehmen
	alphabet [ˈælfəbet]	Alphabet
	number [ˈnʌmbə]	Zahl, Nummer, Anzahl

Skills – Where people are

16	public [ˈpʌblɪk]	öffentlich, Staats…
	holiday [ˈhɒlədeɪ]	Urlaub, Ferien
	public holiday [ˌpʌblɪk ˈhɒlədeɪ]	Feiertag
	trip [trɪp]	Reise, Fahrt
	to be on a business trip [ˌbi ɒn ə ˈbɪznəs trɪp]	auf einer Geschäftsreise sein
	sick [sɪk]	krank, übel
	to be off sick [bi ˈɒf sɪk]	krank (zu Hause) sein
	three [θri:]	drei
	to be on vacation [bi ɒn vəˈkeɪʃn]	im Urlaub sein, in den Ferien sein
	engineer [ˌendʒɪˈnɪə]	Ingenieur/in, Techniker/in
	design engineer [dɪˈzaɪn endʒɪnɪə]	Konstrukteur/in, Entwicklungsingenieur/in
	design assistant [dɪˈzaɪn əsɪstənt]	Designassistent/in
	project assistant [ˈprɒdʒekt əsɪstənt]	Projektassistent/in
	page [peɪdʒ]	Seite, Webseite
	box [bɒks]	Kästchen
	vacation [vəˈkeɪʃn]	Urlaub

Skills - Numbers and spelling

17	spelling ['spelɪŋ]	Rechtschreibung, Schreib-weise
	task [tɑːsk]	Aufgabe
	me [mi, miː]	ich, mich, mir
	back [bæk]	zurück
	to call back [ˌkɔːl 'bæk]	zurückrufen
	of course [ˌəf 'kɔːs]	natürlich, selbstverständlich
	phone number ['fəʊn nʌmbə]	Telefonnummer
	What's your phone number? [ˌwɒts jɔː 'fəʊn nʌmbə]	Wie lautet deine/Ihre Telefonnummer?
	country ['kʌntri]	Land, Landschaft
	area ['eəriə]	Gebiet, Gegend, Ort
	code [kəʊd]	Vorwahl
	country code ['kʌntri kəʊd]	Landesvorwahl
	area code ['eəriə kəʊd]	örtliche Vorwahl
	Mrs ['mɪsɪz]	Frau
	line [laɪn]	Leitung, Telefonanschluss, Linie
	direct [də'rekt]	direkt, unmittelbar
	direct line [dəˌrekt 'laɪn]	Durchwahl
	OK [əʊ'keɪ]	O.K., in Ordnung
	to repeat [rɪ'piːt]	wiederholen
	zero ['zɪərəʊ]	null
	one [wʌn]	eins, ein/e
	four [fɔː]	vier
	five [faɪv]	fünf
	six [sɪks]	sechs
	seven ['sevn]	sieben
	eight [eɪt]	acht
	nine [naɪn]	neun
	to say [seɪ]	sagen, sprechen
	group [gruːp]	Gruppe
	double ['dʌbl]	doppelt, zwei mal, Doppel-
	capital ['kæpɪtl]	groß, Haupt-

Skills - Taking a message

18	to decide [dɪ'saɪd]	entscheiden, beschließen
	man [mæn]	Mann, Mensch
	to put [pʊt]	legen, setzen, stellen
	order ['ɔːdə]	Reihenfolge, Auftrag, Bestellung
	to put in order [ˌpʊt ɪn 'ɔːdə]	in eine Reihenfolge bringen
	I'm sorry. [aɪm 'sɒri]	Tut mir leid.
	to give [gɪv]	geben
	making ['meɪkɪŋ]	Herstellung

	each [iːtʃ]	jede/r/s, je
	to have [həv, hæv]	haben
	nice [naɪs]	schön, nett, gut
	Have a nice day. [həv ə ˌnaɪs 'deɪ]	Einen schönen Tag noch.
	too [tuː]	zu, auch
	help [help]	Hilfe
	Thank you for your help. ['θæŋk ju: fə jɔː 'help]	Vielen Dank für deine/Ihre/eure Hilfe.
	Thank you for calling. ['θæŋk ju: fə 'kɔlɪŋ]	Danke für den Anruf.
	Thank you for your call. ['θæŋk ju: fə jɔː 'kɔːl]	Danke für deinen/Ihren/euren Anruf.
19	to tick [tɪk]	abhaken, ankreuzen
	true [truː]	wahr, richtig
	false [fɔːls]	falsch
	brochure ['brəʊʃə]	Broschüre, Prospekt
	gap [gæp]	Lücke
	to leave [liːv]	verlassen, hinterlassen
	to leave a message [liːv ə 'mesɪdʒ]	eine Nachricht hinterlassen
	later ['leɪtə]	später
	I have that. [aɪ 'hæv ðæt]	Das habe ich verstanden.
	to spell [spel]	buchstabieren, orthografisch richtig schreiben
	town [taʊn]	Stadt
	to come [kʌm]	kommen
	certainly ['sɜːtnli]	sicher, natürlich
20	subject ['sʌbdʒɪkt]	Thema, Subjekt
	object ['ɒbdʒɪkt]	Gegenstand, Objekt
	subject pronoun [ˌsʌbdʒɪkt 'prəʊnaʊn]	Subjektpronomen
	object pronoun [ˌɒbdʒɪkt 'prəʊnaʊn]	Objektpronomen
	us [ʌs]	uns, wir
	them [ðem]	sie, ihnen
	but [bʌt]	aber
	to speak Russian [ˌspiːk 'rʌʃn]	Russisch sprechen
	request [rɪ'kwest]	Bitte
	problem ['prɒbləm]	Problem, Aufgabe
	No problem. [nəʊ 'prɒbləm]	Kein Problem.
	sure [ʃʊə]	sicher
	to be afraid [bi ə'freɪd]	befürchten
	friendly ['frendli]	freundlich
	response [rɪ'spɒns]	Antwort, Reaktion
	like [laɪk]	wie

Grammar Practice

| 21 | to contact [ˈkɒntækt] | kontaktieren, sich in Verbindung setzen mit |
| | mobile [ˈməʊbaɪl] | Handy, Mobiltelefon |

Consolidation

22	to write [raɪt]	schreiben
	down [daʊn]	hinunter, herunter
	to write down [ˌraɪt ˈdaʊn]	aufschreiben
	order number [ˈɔːdə nʌmbə]	Bestellnummer, Auftragsnummer
	it's about [ɪts əˈbaʊt]	es geht um
	there [ðeə]	da, dort, dahin, dorthin
	to change [tʃeɪndʒ]	ändern, tauschen
	role [rəʊl]	Rolle
	sector [ˈsektə]	Bereich

Unit 3 – Around the company

Around the company

23	around, round [əˈraʊnd]	um, herum, rund um
	to see [siː]	sehen, verstehen, besuchen
	photocopier, copier [ˈfəʊtəʊkɒpiə]	Fotokopierer
	plant [plɑːnt]	Pflanze
	to hear [hɪə]	hören, anhören, erfahren
	book [bʊk]	Buch
	chair [tʃeə]	Stuhl
	coffee [ˈkɒfi]	Kaffee
	machine [məˈʃiːn]	Maschine
	coffee machine [ˈkɒfi məʃiːn]	Kaffeemaschine
	desk [desk]	Schreibtisch
	monitor [ˈmɒnɪtə]	Monitor, Bildschirm
	mouse [maʊs]	Maus
	water [ˈwɔːtə]	Wasser
	cool [kuːl]	kühl
	water cooler [ˈwɔːtə kuːlə]	Trinkwasserkühler
	window [ˈwɪndəʊ]	Fenster
	to greet [griːt]	grüßen, begrüßen
	visitor [ˈvɪzɪtə]	Besucher/in
	equipment [ɪˈkwɪpmənt]	Ausrüstung
	office equipment [ˈɒfɪs ɪkwɪpmənt]	Büromaterial, Büroausstattung, Büroeinrichtung
	expression [ɪkˈspreʃn]	Ausdruck
	plural [ˈplʊərəl]	Plural, Mehrzahl

Skills – Meeting and introducing people

24	to excuse [ɪkˈskjuːz]	entschuldigen
	Excuse me. [ɪkˈskjuːs mi]	Entschuldigung.
	coat [kəʊt]	Mantel, Jacke
	to please [pliːz]	zufriedenstellen
	friend [frend]	Freund/in, Bekannte/r
	person [ˈpɜːsn]	Mensch, Person
	bad [bæd]	schlecht
	Not bad. [ˌnɒt ˈbæd]	Nicht schlecht.

Skills – Can I show you around?

25	to show [ʃəʊ]	zeigen, vorzeigen
	around [raʊnd]	(rund)herum
	to show around [ʃəʊ ˈraʊnd]	herumführen
	head [hed]	Kopf, Leiter/in
	head office [ˌhed ˈɒfɪs]	Hauptsitz, Zentrale
	big [bɪg]	groß
	well [wel]	also, nun, gut
	floor [flɔː]	Etage, Stockwerk
	plan [plæn]	Plan
	floor plan [ˈflɔː plæn]	Etagenplan
	reception [rɪˈsepʃn]	Rezeption, Empfang
	production area [prəˈdʌkʃn eəriə]	Produktionsbereich, Herstellungsbereich
	over [ˈəʊvə]	über
	over here [ˌəʊvə ˈhɪə]	hier drüben
	along [əˈlɒŋ]	entlang
	along here [əˌlɒŋ ˈhɪə]	hier entlang
	left [left]	links, nach links
	on the left [ɒn ðə ˈleft]	links, auf der linken Seite
	on the right [ɒn ðə ˈraɪt]	rechts, auf der rechten Seite
	to mention [ˈmenʃn]	erwähnen
	yellow [ˈjeləʊ]	gelb
	colour [ˈkʌlə]	Farbe
	red [red]	rot
	pink [pɪŋk]	rosa
	purple [ˈpɜːpl]	lila
	orange [ˈɒrɪndʒ]	orange
	green [griːn]	grün
	black [blæk]	schwarz
	grey [greɪ]	grau
	need [niːd]	brauchen, nötig haben, erfordern
	WC [ˌdʌbljuː ˈsiː]	WC, Toilette
	rest [rest]	Ruhe, Pause
	restroom [ˈrestruːm]	Toilette
	toilet [ˈtɔɪlət]	Toilette
	bathroom [ˈbɑːθruːm]	Badezimmer, Toilette
	way [weɪ]	Weg, Richtung

This way, please. ['ðɪs   Hier entlang bitte.

tour [tʊə]   Tour, Rundgang
between [bɪ'twi:n]   zwischen
opposite ['ɒpəzɪt]   gegenüber
conference ['kɒnfərəns]   Konferenz, Besprechung
room ['ru:m]   Raum
conference room   Konferenzraum
    ['kɒnfərəns ru:m]
next to ['neksttə]   neben
human ['hju:mən]   menschlich
resources [rɪ'zɔ:sɪz]   Mittel, Ressourcen
HR = human resources   personelle Mittel, Personal
    [ˌeɪtʃ 'ɑ:; ˌhju:mən
    rɪ'zɔ:sɪz]
administration   Verwaltung
    [ədˌmɪnɪ'streɪʃn]
purchasing ['pɜ:tʃəsɪŋ]   Einkauf
sale [seɪl]   Verkauf
warehouse ['weəhaʊs]   Lager, Lagerhalle
finance ['faɪnæns]   Geld, Finanzwesen

Skills – Describing locations

26   sales department ['seɪlz   Verkaufsabteilung
    dɪpɑ:tmənt]
to describe [dɪ'skraɪb]   beschreiben
location [ləʊ'keɪʃn]   Lage, Ort, Platz
childcare ['tʃaɪldkeə]   Kinderbetreuung
centre (BrE), center   Anlage, Einrichtung,
    (AmE) ['sentə]   Center
childcare centre   Kinderbetreuungs-
    ['tʃaɪldkeə sentə]   einrichtung
human resources   Personalabteilung
    department [ˌhju:mən
    rɪ'zɔ:sɪz dɪpɑ:tmənt]
finance department   Finanzabteilung
    ['faɪnæns dɪpɑ:tmənt]
power point ['paʊə   Power Point™, Steckdose
    pɔɪnt]
projector [pre'dʒektə]   Projektor
wall [wɔ:l]   Wand, Mauer
whiteboard ['waɪtbɔ:d]   Weißwandtafel, weiße Tafel
reception area [rɪ'sepʃn   Empfangsbereich
    eəriə]
sport [spɔ:t]   Sport, Sportart
facility [fə'sɪləti]   Anlage
sports facilities ['spɔ:ts   Sportanlagen, Sportplatz
    fəsɪləti:z]
car [kɑ:]   Auto, Wagen
park [pɑ:k]   Park
to park [pɑ:k]   parken
car park ['kɑ: pɑ:k]   Parkplatz, Parkhaus
lot [lɒt]   Menge, Gelände

parking lot ['pɑ:kɪŋ lɒt]   Parkplatz
any ['eni]   (irgend)ein(e/er/s), jede/
    r/s beliebige
staff [stɑ:f]   Personal
restaurant ['restrɒnt]   Restaurant
shop [ʃɒp]   Laden, Geschäft
very ['veri]   sehr
Very nice. [ˌveri 'naɪs]   Sehr schön., Sehr gut.
high [haɪ]   hoch, groß
speed [spi:d]   Geschwindigkeit
high-speed internet   Hochgeschwindigkeits-
    [haɪ ˌspi:d 'ɪntənet]   Internetverbindung
printer ['prɪntə]   Drucker
table ['teɪbl]   Tisch
extra ['ekstrə]   Extra…, zusätzlich
paper ['peɪpə]   Papier
there's [ðeəz]   es gibt, da ist
front [frʌnt]   Vorderseite
in front of [ɪn 'frʌnt əv]   vor
corner ['kɔ:nə]   Ecke
in the corner [ɪn ðə   in der Ecke
    'kɔ:nə]
behind [bɪ'haɪnd]   hinter
under ['ʌndə]   unter
control [kən'trəʊl]   Kontrolle
panel ['pænl]   Kontrolltafel, Schalttafel
control panel [kən'trəʊl   Bedienfeld
    pænl]
air [eə]   Luft
air conditioning ['eə   Klimaanlage,
    kəndɪʃənɪŋ]   Lüftungsanlage
all [ɔ:l]   alles, alle
That's all. [ˌðæts 'ɔ:l]   Das ist alles.
great [greɪt]   groß, super
to think [θɪŋk]   denken, glauben
document ['dɒkjumənt]   Dokument, Textdatei
address [ə'dres]   Adresse, Anschrift
27   blinds [blaɪnds]   Rollo, Jalousie
mini ['mɪnɪ]   sehr klein
loudspeaker   Lautsprecher
    [ˌlaʊd'spi:kə]
beamer ['bi:mə]   Projektor
ceiling ['si:lɪŋ]   Decke
perfect ['pɜ:fɪkt]   perfekt, fehlerfrei
presentation   Präsentation, Vortrag
    [ˌprezn'teɪʃn]
as [əz, æz]   wie, so wie, als
ten [ten]   zehn
pointer ['pɔɪntə]   Zeiger
I see. [aɪ 'si:]   Ich verstehe., Verstanden.
middle ['mɪdl]   Mitte
in the middle (of) [ɪn   in der Mitte (von)
    ðə 'mɪdl]

	to **draw** [drɔː]	zeichnen

Unit 4 – Colleagues and Companies

Colleagues and companies

31	**sketch** [sketʃ]	Skizze
	map [mæp]	Plan, Karte
	sketch map [ˈsketʃ mæp]	gezeichnete Karte
	nationality [ˌnæʃəˈnæləti]	Staatsangehörigkeit, Nationalität
	to **exchange** [ɪksˈtʃeɪndʒ]	austauschen, tauschen, wechseln
	fact [fækt]	Tatsache, Wahrheit
	company facts [ˈkʌmpəni fækts]	Geschäftszahlen

Skills – Business contacts

32	**contact** [ˈkɒntækt]	Kontakt
	business contacts [ˈbɪznəs kɒntækts]	Geschäftskontakte
	customer [ˈkʌstəmə]	Kunde/Kundin
	supplier [səˈplaɪə]	Lieferant/in
	to **supply** [səˈplaɪ]	liefern
	to **buy** [baɪ]	kaufen
	to **sell** [sel]	verkaufen
	cell [sel]	Zelle, Handy
	cell phone [ˈselfəʊn]	Mobiltelefon, Handy
	mobile phone [ˌməʊbaɪl ˈfəʊn]	Mobiltelefon, Handy
	activity [ækˈtɪvəti]	Aktivität, Beschäftigung
	to **manufacture** [ˌmænjuˈfæktʃə]	herstellen, produzieren, fertigen
	to **produce** [prəˈdjuːs]	herstellen, produzieren
	to **make** [meɪk]	machen, herstellen
	also [ˈɔːlsəʊ]	auch, außerdem
	Hightime Electronics [ˈhaɪtaɪm ɪlektrɒnɪks]	Firmenname
	factory [ˈfæktri]	Fabrik
	electronic [ɪˌlekˈtrɒnɪk]	elektronisch
	component [kəmˈpəʊnənt]	Teil, Komponente

Skills – Exchanging information

33	to **highlight** [ˈhaɪlaɪt]	unterstreichen
	to **specialize** [ˈspeʃəlaɪz]	sich spezialisieren
	really [ˈriːəli]	wirklich, sehr
	much [mʌtʃ]	viel
	underscore [ˈʌndəskɔː]	Unterstrich
	dot [dɒt]	Punkt
	interesting [ˈɪntrəstɪŋ]	interessant
	more [mɔː]	mehr
	type [taɪp]	Art, Sorte

	at the side [ət ðə ˈsaɪd]	an der Seite
	video [ˈvɪdiəʊ]	Video
	video conference [ˈvɪdiəʊ kɒnfərəns]	Videokonferenz
	to **install** [ɪnˈstɔːl]	installieren, einbauen
	microphone [ˈmaɪkrəfəʊn]	Mikrofon
	everything [ˈevriθɪŋ]	alles
28	**singular** [ˈsɪŋgjələ]	Singular, Einzahl
	noun [naʊn]	Substantiv, Nomen
	most [məʊst]	der/die/das meiste, die meisten
	to **end** [end]	enden, beenden
	ending [ˈendɪŋ]	Ende, Endung
	lunch [lʌntʃ]	Mittagessen
	fax [fæks]	Fax
	consonant [ˈkɒnsənənt]	Konsonant
	copy [ˈkɒpi]	Kopie
	irregular [ɪˈregjələ]	unregelmäßig
	child [tʃaɪld]	Kind
	woman [ˈwʊmən]	Frau

Grammar Practice

29	**comfortable** [ˈkʌmftəbl]	bequem
	lift [lɪft]	Fahrstuhl, Aufzug
	businesswoman [ˈbɪznəswʊmən]	Geschäftsfrau
	businessman [ˈbɪznəsmən]	Geschäftsmann
	construction [kənˈstrʌkʃn]	Bau, Konstruktion
	seminar [ˈsemɪnɑː]	Seminar
	sales manager [ˈseɪlz mænɪdʒə]	Verkaufsleiter/in
	video conference facilities [ˌvɪdiəʊ kɒnfərəns fəˈsɪlətis]	technische Anlage für eine Videokonferenz

Consolidation

30	**web** [web]	(World Wide) Web
	web address [web əˈdres]	Web-Adresse
	sunny [ˈsʌni]	sonnig
	pen [pen]	Stift
	classroom [ˈklɑːsruːm]	Klassenzimmer
	to **get** [get]	bekommen, werden, kommen
	garden [ˈgɑːdn]	Garten
	building [ˈbɪldɪŋ]	Gebäude
	purchasing department [ˈpɜːtʃəsɪŋ dɪpɑːtmənt]	Abteilung Einkauf

plc = public limited company [ˌpiːelˈsiː; ˌpʌblɪk ˌlɪmɪtɪd ˈkʌmpəni]	Aktiengesellschaft	
Inc. [ɪŋk]	eingetragen	
Corp. = Corporation [ˌkɔːpəˈreɪʃn]	Konzern, Handelsgesellschaft	
Ltd = Limited [ˈlɪmɪtɛd]	GmbH	
hyphen [ˈhaɪfn]	Bindestrich, Trennstrich	
sales representative [ˈseɪlz reprɪzentətɪv]	Vertreter/in	
hardware [ˈhɑːdweə]	Hardware	
hardware department [ˈhɑːdweə dɪpɑːtmənt]	Hardware-Abteilung	
road [rəʊd]	Straße	
very much [ˌveri ˈmʌtʃ]	sehr	

Skills – You and your company

34	**special** [ˈspeʃl]	Sonder-, speziell
	offer [ˈɒfə]	Angebot
	dear [dɪə]	lieb, Liebe/r …
	first [fɜːst]	zuerst
	to **let** [let]	lassen
	myself [maɪˈself]	mich
	to **operate** [ˈɒpəreɪt]	arbeiten, in Betrieb sein
	operation [ˌɒpəˈreɪʃn]	Betrieb
	module [ˈmɒdjuːl]	Modul, Baustein
	to **coordinate** [kəʊˈɔːdɪneɪt]	koordinieren, aufeinander abstimmen
	beginning [bɪˈgɪnɪŋ]	Beginn, Anfang
	main [meɪn]	Haupt…
	PR = public relations [ˌpiːˈɑː; ˌpʌblɪk rɪˈleɪʃns]	Öffentlichkeitsarbeit, Werbung
	active [ˈæktɪv]	aktiv, tätig
	to **be active in** [bi ˈæktɪv ɪn]	aktiv sein, vertreten sein
	branch [brɑːntʃ]	Geschäftszweig, Filiale
	product [ˈprɒdʌkt]	Produkt
	to **organize** [ˈɔːgənaɪz]	organisieren
	to **plan** [plæn]	planen, vorhaben
	sheet [ʃiːt]	Blatt
	fact sheet [ˈfækt ʃiːt]	Datenblatt
	exercise [ˈeksəsaɪz]	Übung
	invitation [ˌɪnvɪˈteɪʃn]	Einladung
35	**employee** [ɪmˈplɔɪiː]	Arbeitnehmer/in, Beschäftigte/r, Angestellte/r
	large [lɑːdʒ]	groß
	global [ˈgləʊbl]	weltweit, global
	north [nɔːθ]	Norden
	south [saʊθ]	Süden
	audience [ˈɔːdiəns]	Publikum

	some [səm, sʌm]	etwas, einige, ungefähr
	many [ˈmeni]	viele
	how many [haʊ ˈmeni]	wie viele
	cubic [ˈkjuːbɪk]	Kubik…, kubisch
	metre [ˈmiːtə]	Meter
	cubic metre [ˈkjuːbɪk miːtə]	Kubikmeter
	year [jɪə]	Jahr
	wood [wʊd]	Holz
	door [dɔː]	Tür
	market [ˈmɑːkɪt]	Markt
	fabric [ˈfæbrɪk]	Stoff, Gewebe
	to **receive** [rɪˈsiːv]	erhalten, bekommen
	to **become** [bɪˈkʌm]	werden
	boss [bɒs]	Chef/in, Boss
	chef [ʃef]	Küchenchef/in, Koch/Köchin
	to **control** [kənˈtrəʊl]	beherrschen
	handy [ˈhændi]	nützlich, praktisch
36	**simple present** [ˌsɪmpl ˈpreznt]	einfache Form der Gegenwart, Präsens
	routine [ruːˈtiːn]	Routine, Gewohnheit
	routine activity [ruːˈtiːn æktɪvəti]	Routinehandlung
	to **live** [lɪv]	leben, wohnen
	when [wen]	wann, wenn
	to **start** [stɑːt]	anfangen, beginnen
	why [waɪ]	warum, weshalb
	after [ˈɑːftə]	nach, hinter

Grammar Practice

37	**electrical** [ɪˈlektrɪkl]	elektrisch, Elektro…
	electrical products [ɪˌlektrɪkl ˈprɒdʌkts]	Elektrogeräte
	client [ˈklaɪənt]	Kunde/Kundin, Klient/in
	major [ˈmeɪdʒə]	groß, bedeutend
	MP3 player [ˌem piː ˈθriː pleɪə]	MP3-Spieler
	portable [ˈpɔːtəbl]	tragbar
	DVD [ˌdiːviːˈdiː]	DVD, digital versatile disc
	DVD player [ˌdiːviːˈdiː pleɪə]	DVD-Spieler
	Head of Sales [ˌhed əv ˈseɪlz]	Abteilungseiter/in
	often [ˈɒfn]	oft, häufig
	to **travel** [ˈtrævl]	reisen, fahren
	production worker [prəˈdʌkʃn wɜːkə]	Produktionsarbeiter/in
	industry [ˈɪndəstri]	Industrie, Branche
	eastern [ˈiːstən]	östlich, Ost…

Consolidation

38	**called** [kɔːld]	namens, mit dem Namen
	favourite [ˈfeɪvərɪt]	Lieblings…

Unit 5 – Work schedules

Work schedules

39 **schedule** [ˈʃedjuːl]   Zeitplan

work schedule [ˈwɜːk ʃedjuːl]   Arbeitsplan

regularly [ˈregjələli]   regelmäßig, oft

idea [aɪˈdɪə]   Idee, Plan

every [ˈevri]   jede/r/s

iPod [ˈaɪpɒd]   iPod

to **watch** [wɒtʃ]   schauen, zuschauen

YouTube [ˈjuːtjuːb]   YouTube

newsletter [ˈnjuːzletə]   Rundschreiben, Newsletter

free [friː]   frei, kostenlos

time [taɪm]   Zeit, Mal

free time [ˌfriː ˈtaɪm]   Freizeit

yoga [ˈjəʊgə]   Yoga

hour [ˈaʊə]   Stunde, Zeit

lunch hour [ˈlʌntʃ aʊə]   Mittagspause

to **eat** [iːt]   essen

home [həʊm]   Zuhause, Wohnung

at home [ət ˈhəʊm]   zu Hause

bread [bred]   Brot

bread shop [ˈbred ʃɒp]   Bäckerei

soup [suːp]   Suppe

pasta [ˈpæstə]   Nudeln

salad [ˈsæləd]   Salat

hot [hɒt]   heiß, warm

sandwich [ˈsænwɪtʃ]   Sandwich

music [ˈmjuːzɪk]   Musik

hip-hop music [ˈhɪp hɒp mjuːzɪk]   Hip-Hop-Musik

newspaper [ˈnjuːzpeɪpə]   Zeitung

to **talk** [tɔːk]   reden, sprechen, sich unterhalten

radio [ˈreɪdɪəʊ]   Radio

week [wiːk]   Woche

how often [həʊ ˈɒfn]   wie oft?

usually [ˈjuːʒʊəli]   normalerweise, gewöhnlich

sometimes [ˈsʌmtaɪmz]   manchmal

never [ˈnevə]   nie, niemals

to **love** [lʌv]   lieben

I like doing … [aɪ ˌlaɪk ˈduːɪŋ]   Ich mache/tue gerne …

I love doing … [aɪ ˌlʌv ˈduːɪŋ]   Ich mache/tue gerne …

Skills – Routines

40 **past** [pɑːst]   nach

quarter [ˈkwɔːtə]   Viertel

a quarter past [ə ˈkwɔːtə pɑːst]   Viertel nach

a quarter to [ə ˈkwɔːtə tə]   Viertel vor

half [hɑːf]   halb

half past [ˈhɑːf pɑːst]   halb (Uhrzeit)

pm [ˌpiː ˈem]   nachmittags, abends (lat. post meridiem)

breakfast [ˈbrekfəst]   Frühstück

to **have breakfast** [ˌhəv ˈbrekfəst]   frühstücken

before [bɪˈfɔː]   bevor, vor

last [lɑːst]   letzte/r/s

together [təˈgeðə]   zusammen

last time [ˈlɑːst taɪm]   letztes Mal

canteen [kænˈtiːn]   Kantine

overtime [ˈəʊvətaɪm]   Überstunden

to **work overtime** [wɜːk ˈəʊvətaɪm]   Überstunden machen

early [ˈɜːli]   früh, zeitig

to **switch on** [ˌswɪtʃ ˈɒn]   anschalten

to **switch off** [ˌswɪtʃ ˈɒf]   ausschalten

to **do overtime** [du ˈəʊvətaɪm]   Überstunden machen

because [bɪˈkɒz]   weil, denn

family [ˈfæməli]   Familie

break [breɪk]   Pause

breakfast break [ˈbrekfəst breɪk]   Frühstückspause

to **finish** [ˈfɪnɪʃ]   fertig sein, beenden, aufhören

eleven [ɪˈlevn]   elf

twelve [twelv]   zwölf

thirteen [ˌθɜːˈtiːn]   dreizehn

fourteen [ˌfɔːˈtiːn]   vierzehn

fifteen [ˌfɪfˈtiːn]   fünfzehn

sixteen [ˌsɪksˈtiːn]   sechzehn

seventeen [ˌsevnˈtiːn]   siebzehn

eighteen [ˌeɪˈtiːn]   achtzehn

nineteen [ˌnaɪnˈtiːn]   neunzehn

twenty [ˈtwenti]   zwanzig

thirty [ˈθɜːti]   dreißig

forty [ˈfɔːti]   vierzig

fifty [ˈfɪfti]   fünfzig

sixty [ˈsɪksti]   sechzig

seventy [ˈsevnti]   siebzig

eighty [ˈeɪti]   achtzig

ninety [ˈnaɪnti]   neunzig

hundred [ˈhʌndrəd]   hundert

41 **What time is it?** [wɒt ˈtaɪm ɪz ɪt]   Wie spät ist es?

am [ˌeɪ ˈem]   morgens, vormittags (lat. ante meridiem)

in the morning [ɪn ðə ˈmɔːnɪŋ]	morgens, am Morgen
in the afternoon [ɪn ðiː ˌɑːftəˈnuːn]	nachmittags, am Nach-mittag
competition [ˌkɒmpəˈtɪʃn]	Konkurrenz, Wettbewerb
to win [wɪn]	gewinnen
must [məst, mʌst]	müssen
smartphone [ˈsmɑːtfəʊn]	Smartphone
entry [ˈentri]	Eintrag
lifeline [ˈlaɪflaɪn]	hier: Verbindung
girlfriend [ˈgɜːlfrend]	Freundin
normal [ˈnɔːml]	normal, üblich
only [ˈəʊnli]	einzige/r/s
to keep [kiːp]	halten, bewahren
touch [tʌtʃ]	Verbindung
to stay [steɪ]	bleiben, wohnen
to keep in touch [kiːp ɪn ˈtʌtʃ]	in Verbindung bleiben
to stay in touch [ˌsteɪ ɪn ˈtʌtʃ]	in Verbindung bleiben
to sort [sɔːt]	sortieren
post [pəʊst]	Post
photocopy [ˈfəʊtəʊkɒpi]	Fotokopie
to make photocopies [meɪk ˈfəʊtəʊkɒpis]	fotokopieren
quite [kwaɪt]	ziemlich, völlig
different [ˈdɪfrənt]	unterschiedlich, verschie-den
to want [wʌnt]	wollen, mögen, brauchen
fresh [freʃ]	neu, frisch
supermarket [ˈsuːpəmɑːkɪt]	Supermarkt
cup [kʌp]	Tasse
tea [tiː]	Tee
a cup of tea [ə kʌp əv ˈtiː]	eine Tasse Tee
apple [ˈæpl]	Apfel
banana [bəˈnɑːnə]	Banane
working day [ˈwɜːkɪŋ deɪ]	Arbeitstag
always [ˈɔːlweɪz]	immer
online [ˌɒnˈlaɪn]	online, Online…
to go online [gəʊ ɒnˈlaɪn]	ins Internet gehen
news [njuːz]	Nachricht/en
hobby [ˈhɒbi]	Hobby
local [ˈləʊkl]	örtlich
club [klʌb]	Klub, Verein
sports club [ˈspɔːts klʌb]	Sportverein
lunchtime [ˈlʌntʃtaɪm]	Mittagszeit
end [end]	Ende
to go to bed [gəʊ tə ˈbed]	ins Bett gehen, schlafen gehen
to sleep [sliːp]	schlafen
until [ʌnˈtɪl]	bis
from … to … [frəm … tə]	von … bis …
about [əˈbaʊt]	circa
meal [miːl]	Mahlzeit, Essen
TV [ˌtiːˈviː]	Fernsehen, Fernseher
to watch TV [wɒtʃ ˌtiːˈvi]	fernsehen
house [haʊs]	Haus
lesson [ˈlesn]	Unterricht, Lektion
midday [ˌmɪdˈdeɪ]	Mittag
to update [ˌʌpˈdeɪt]	auf den neuesten Stand bringen, aktualisieren
late [leɪt]	spät
o'clock [əˈklɒk]	Uhr
at nine o'clock [ət naɪn əˈklɒk]	um 9 Uhr

Skills – Work-life balance

42 **life** [laɪf]	Leben
balance [ˈbæləns]	Gleichgewicht, Ausgegli-chenheit
work-life balance [ˌwɜːk ˈlaɪf bæləns]	Work-Life-Balance
capital city [ˌkæpɪtl ˈsɪti]	Hauptstadt, hier: Firmen-name
ex [eks]	Ex
ex-colleague [eksˈkɒliːg]	Exkollege/in
lunch break [ˈlʌntʃ breɪk]	Mittagspause
hard [hɑːd]	hart
to work hard [ˌwɜːk ˈhɑːd]	hart arbeiten
into [ˈɪntə, ˈɪntu, ˈɪntuː]	in, hinein
again [əˈgen, əˈgeɪn]	noch einmal
long [lɒŋ]	lang, weit, lange
minute [ˈmɪnɪt]	Minute, Moment
movie [ˈmuːvi]	Film
to go to a movie [gəʊ tu ə ˈmuːvi]	ins Kino gehen
to jog [dʒɒg]	joggen
to go jogging [gəʊ ˈdʒɒgɪŋ]	joggen gehen
to exercise [ˈeksəsaɪz]	trainieren
Monday [ˈmʌndeɪ]	Montag
Tuesday [ˈtjuːzdeɪ]	Dienstag
Wednesday [ˈwenzdeɪ]	Mittwoch
Thursday [ˈθɜːzdeɪ]	Donnerstag

Saturday [ˈsætədeɪ]	Samstag
Sunday [ˈsʌndeɪ]	Sonntag
what about ... [ˌwɒt əˈbaʊt]	was ist mit ...
except [ɪkˈsept]	außer, ausgenommen
on Monday(s) [ɒn ˈmʌndeɪz]	Montag, montags
weekend [wikˈend]	Wochenende
once [wʌns]	einmal, einst, früher einmal
once a week [ˌwʌns ə ˈwiːk]	einmal in der Woche
to **drink** [drɪŋk]	trinken
twice [twaɪs]	zweimal
three times a day [θriː ˌtaɪms ə ˈdeɪ]	dreimal am Tag

Skills – Talking about free time

43	**husband** [ˈhʌzbənd]	Mann, Ehemann
	to **enjoy** [ɪnˈdʒɔɪ]	genießen
	full [fʊl]	voll, komplett
	full-time [ˈfʊl taɪm]	Vollzeit
	part-time [ˌpaːt ˈtaɪm]	Teilzeit
	producer [prəˈdjuːsə]	Hersteller/in, Produzent/in
	music producer [ˌmjuːzɪk prəˈdjuːsə]	Musikproduzent/in
	to **manage** [ˈmænɪdʒ]	leiten, führen, managen
	to **manage the house** [ˌmænɪdʒ ðə ˈhaʊs]	den Haushalt machen
	to **come home** [kʌm ˈhəʊm]	nach Hause kommen
	eating out [ˌitɪŋ ˈaʊt]	essen gehen, ins Restaurant gehen
	in the evenings [ɪn ði ˈiːvnɪŋs]	abends
	to **play** [pleɪ]	spielen
	walk [wɔːk]	Spaziergang, Wanderung
	to **go for a walk** [ˌgəʊ fər ə ˈwɔːk]	spazieren gehen
	cinema [sɪnəmə]	Kino
	to **go to the cinema** [ˌgəʊ tə ðə ˈsɪnəmə]	ins Kino gehen
	theatre [ˈθɪətə]	Theater
	concert [ˈkɒnsət]	Konzert
	student [ˈstjuːdnt]	Student/in, Kursteilnehmer/in
	squash [skwɒʃ]	Squash
	cycling [ˈsaɪklɪŋ]	Radfahren
	gym [dʒɪm]	Fitnesscenter
	shopping [ˈʃɒpɪŋ]	Einkaufen, Einkäufe
	game [geɪm]	Spiel

	computer game	Computerspiel
	football [ˈfʊtbɔːl]	Fußball, Football
	tennis [ˈtenɪs]	Tennis
	chess [tʃes]	Schach
	gardening [ˈgaːdnɪŋ]	Gartenarbeit
	to **prefer** [prɪˈfɜː]	vorziehen, etwas lieber tun
	sporty [ˈspɔːti]	sportlich
44	**AOL** [eɪəʊ ˈel]	Firmenname
	to **form** [fɔːm]	formulieren, bilden
	to **hate** [heɪt]	hassen
	adverb [ˈædvɜːb]	Adverb
	frequency [ˈfriːkwənsi]	Häufigkeit, Frequenz
	normally [ˈnɔːməli]	normalerweise, gewöhnlich
	rarely [ˈreəli]	selten

Grammar Practice

45	**wrong** [rɒŋ]	falsch
	to **work very long hours** [ˌwɜːk ˌveri lɒŋ ˈaʊəz]	sehr lange arbeiten
	stress [stres]	Stress, Belastung
	night [naɪt]	Nacht, Abend
	clip [klɪp]	Clip, Ausschnitt
	video clip [ˈvɪdiəʊklɪp]	Videoclip
	fashionista [ˌfæʃnˈiːstə]	Trendsetter/in
	fashion [ˈfæʃn]	Trend, Mode
	fashion-design company [ˌfæʃn dɪzaɪn ˈkʌmpəni]	Modedesign-Firma
	jeans [dʒiːnz]	Jeans
	coffee break [ˈkɒfibreɪk]	Kaffeepause
	to **compare** [kəmˈpeə]	vergleichen
	same [seɪm]	der/die/das gleiche
	position [pəˈzɪʃn]	Position, Lage, Standpunkt

Consolidation

46	**taxi** [ˈtæksi]	Taxi
	bicycle [ˈbaɪsɪkl]	Fahrrad
	taxi bicycle [ˈtæksi baɪsɪkl]	Fahrradtaxi
	to **report** [rɪˈpɔːt]	berichten
	month [mʌnθ]	Monat
	how long [haʊ ˈlɒŋ]	wie lange
	to **find out** [faɪnd ˈaʊt]	herausfinden
	Google [ˈguːgl]	Firmenname
	to **offer** [ˈɒfə]	anbieten

Unit 6 – Reviews and reports

Reviews and reports

47	**review** [rɪˈvjuː]	Überprüfung, Rezension
	report [rɪˈpɔːt]	Bericht

headline ['hedlaɪn]	Schlagzeile, Überschrift	
excerpt ['eksɜːpt]	Auszug, Ausschnitt	
policy ['pɒləsi]	Politik, Grundsatz	
May [meɪ]	Mai	
to **open** ['əʊpən]	aufmachen, öffnen	
sales administration center [ˌseɪlzədmɪnɪ'streɪʃn sentə]	Abteilung für Auftragsabwicklung	
hit [hɪt]	Erfolg	
June [dʒuːn]	Juni	
July [dʒu'laɪ]	Juli	
September [sep'tembə]	September	
mid [ˌmɪd]	Mitte	
summer ['sʌmə]	Sommer	
mid-summer [ˌmɪd'sʌmə]	Mittsommer, Hochsommer	
party ['pɑːti]	Party	
chief [tʃiːf]	Chef...	
financial [faɪ'nænʃl]	Finanz..., finanziell	
officer ['ɒfɪsə]	Beamter/Beamtin	
chief financial officer [ˌtʃiːf faɪ'nænʃl ɒfɪsə]	Leiter/in der Finanzabteilung	
performance [pə'fɔːməns]	Leistung	
performance review [pə'fɔːməns rɪvjuː]	Leistungsüberblick	
feedback ['fiːdbæk]	Feedback, Rückmeldung	
for the first time [fə ðə 'fɜːst taɪm]	zum ersten Mal	
date [deɪt]	Datum	
past [pɑːst]	Vergangenheit	
to **give a report** [gɪv ə rɪ'pɔːt]	berichten, einen Bericht abgeben	
regular ['regjələ]	regelmäßig, normal	
ordinal ['ɔːdɪnl]	Ordinal-, Ordnungs-	

Skills - Was it a good year?

48	to **give 100%** [gɪv wʌn ˌhʌndrəd pə'sent]	100 Prozent geben
	thousand ['θaʊznd]	tausend
	tomorrow [tə'mɒrəʊ]	morgen
	yesterday ['jestədeɪ]	gestern
	method ['meθəd]	Methode
	yesterday's methods [jestədeɪz 'meθəds]	überholte Methoden, Methoden von gestern
	still [stɪl]	immer noch
	old [əʊld]	alt, ehemalig
	tgif = Thank God It's Friday! [tiː dʒiː aɪ 'ef; θæŋk ˌgɒd ɪts 'fraɪdeɪ]	Zum Glück ist bald Wochenende!
	God [gɒd]	Gott

	bankrupt ['bæŋkrʌpt]	bankrott
	Berlin Wall [bɜːˌlɪn 'wɔːl]	Berliner Mauer
	IBM [aɪ biː 'em]	Firmenname
	launch [lɔːntʃ]	Einführung, Präsentation
	January ['dʒænjuəri]	Januar
	February ['februəri]	Februar
	March [mɑːtʃ]	März
	April ['eɪprəl]	April
	August ['ɔːgəst]	August
	October [ɒk'təʊbə]	Oktober
	November [nəʊ'vembə]	November
	December [dɪ'sembə]	Dezember
	second ['sekənd]	zweite/r/s
	third [θɜːd]	dritte/r/s
	fourth [fɔːθ]	vierte/r/s
	fifth [fɪfθ]	fünfte/r/s
	sixth [sɪksθ]	sechste/r/s
	seventh ['sevnθ]	siebte/r/s
	eighth [eɪtθ]	achte/r/s
	ninth [naɪnθ]	neunte/r/s
	tenth [tenθ]	zehnte/r/s
	eleventh [ɪ'levnθ]	elfte/r/s
	twelfth [twelfθ]	zwölfte/r/s
	thirteenth [ˌθɜː'tiːnθ]	dreizehnte/r/s
	fourteenth [ˌfɔː'tinθ]	vierzehnte/r/s
	fifteenth [ˌfɪf'tiːnθ]	fünfzehnte/r/s
	sixteenth [ˌsɪks'tiːnθ]	sechzehnte/r/s
	seventeenth [ˌsevn'tiːnθ]	siebzehnte/r/s
	eighteenth [ˌeɪ'tiːnθ]	achtzehnte/r/s
	nineteenth [naɪn'tiːnθ]	neunzehnte/r/s
	twentieth ['twentiəθ]	zwanzigste/r/s
	thirtieth ['θɜːtiəθ]	dreißigste/r/s
	birthday ['bɜːθdeɪ]	Geburtstag
	spring [sprɪŋ]	Frühling
	autumn ['ɔːtəm]	Herbst
	fall [fɔːl]	Herbst
	winter ['wɪntə]	Winter
	to **identify** [aɪ'dentɪfaɪ]	identifizieren, feststellen
	brother ['brʌðə]	Bruder
49	**article** ['ɑːtɪkl]	Artikel
	system ['sɪstəm]	System
	something ['sʌmθɪŋ]	etwas
	nervous ['nɜːvəs]	nervös, aufgeregt
	unhappy [ʌn'hæpi]	unglücklich, unzufrieden
	those [ðəʊz]	diese
	memory ['meməri]	Gedächtnis, Erinnerung
	memory card ['meməri kɑːd]	Speicherkarte
	important [ɪm'pɔːtnt]	wichtig, einflussreich, bedeutend

to **go on vacation** [gəʊ ɒn vəˈkeɪʃn]   in den Urlaub fahren

possible [ˈpɒsəbl]   möglich

everyone [ˈevriwʌn]   jeder, alle

difficult [ˈdɪfɪkəlt]   schwer, schwierig

external [ɪkˈstɜːnl]   extern, Außen…

service [ˈsɜːvɪs]   Dienst

shareholder [ˈʃeəhəʊldə]   Aktionär/in

happy [ˈhæpi]   glücklich, zufrieden

to **restructure** [ˌriːˈstrʌktʃə]   umstrukturieren

CFO = Chief Financial Officer [ˌsi efˈəʊ; tʃiːf faɪˈnænʃl ɒfɪsə]   Finanzchef/in, Leiter/in der Finanzabteilung

CEO = Chief Executive Officer [ˌsi iːˈəʊ; tʃiːf ɪgˈzekjətɪv ɒfɪsə]   Generaldirektor/in, Geschäftsführer/in, Vorstandsvorsitzende/r

corporate [ˈkɔːpərət]   Unternehmens-, Firmen-

communication [kəˌmjuːnɪˈkeɪʃn]   Kommunikation, Verständigung

workshop [ˈwɜːkʃɒp]   Workshop

hotel [həʊˈtel]   Hotel

to **discuss** [dɪˈskʌs]   besprechen, diskutieren

motivation [ˌməʊtɪˈveɪʃn]   Motivation

top [tɒp]   Spitzen…

consultant [kənˈsʌltənt]   Berater/in

executive [ɪgˈzekjətɪv]   geschäftsführend, leitend

annual [ˈænjuəl]   Jahres…, jährlich, alljährlich

general [ˈdʒenrəl]   allgemein, Haupt…, General…

situation [ˌsɪtʃuˈeɪʃn]   Lage, Situation

Skills – Giving a report

50   to **visit** [ˈvɪzɪt]   besuchen, besichtigen

visit [ˈvɪzɪt]   Besuch, Besichtigung

Fashion Plus [fæʃn ˈplʌs]   Firmenname

to **close** [kləʊz]   schließen, zumachen

to **move** [muːv]   (sich) bewegen, umziehen

ago [əˈgəʊ]   vor

to **stop** [stɒp]   anhalten, aufhören, beenden

change [tʃeɪndʒ]   Änderung, Wechsel

product line [ˈprɒdʌkt laɪn]   Produktlinie

young [jʌŋ]   jung

portfolio [pɔːtˈfəʊliəʊ]   Mappe

attractive [əˈtræktɪv]   attraktiv, ansprechend

stylish [ˈstaɪlɪʃ]   modisch, stilvoll

discussion [dɪˈskʌʃn]   Besprechung, Diskussion

strategy [ˈstrætədʒi]   Strategie

figure [ˈfɪgə]   Zahl

sales figure [ˈseɪlz fɪgə]   Verkaufszahl

delivery [dɪˈlɪvəri]   Zustellung, Lieferung

informed [ɪnˈfɔːmd]   informiert

to **join** [dʒɔɪn]   sich anschließen

success [səkˈses]   Erfolg

Skills – Writing emails

51   **PA = Personal Assistant** [pi ˈeɪ; ˌpɜːsənl əˈsɪstənt]   persönliche/r Assistent/in

soon [suːn]   bald

asap = as soon as possible [ˌeɪ es eɪ ˈpiː; əz ˌsuːn əz ˈpɒsəbl]   baldmöglichst, so bald wie möglich

letter [ˈletə]   Buchstabe

FP = Fashion Plus [ef piː; fæʃn ˈplʌs]   Firmenname

would [wʊd]   würde, wollen

could [kəd, kʊd]   konnte, dürfte, könnte

senior [ˈsiːniə]   ranghöher, dienstälter

to **give a presentation** [gɪv ə ˌpreznˈteɪʃn]   eine Präsentation halten

management [ˈmænɪdʒmənt]   Führung, Management

helpful [ˈhelpfl]   hilfreich, hilfsbereit

clear [klɪə]   klar, offensichtlich

structure [ˈstrʌktʃə]   Struktur, Aufbau

successful [səkˈsesfl]   erfolgreich

to **include** [ɪnˈkluːd]   einschließen, einbeziehen

detail [ˈdiːteɪl]   Einzelheit, Detail

on Monday morning [ɒn ˌmʌndeɪ ˈmɔːnɪŋ]   am Montagmorgen

reply [rɪˈplaɪ]   Antwort

Head of Design [ˌhed əv dɪˈzaɪn]   Leiter/in der Designabteilung

if [ɪf]   falls, wenn

formal [ˈfɔːml]   förmlich, offiziell, formal

neutral [ˈnjuːtrəl]   neutral, unbeteiligt

further [ˈfɜːðə]   weitere/r/s

to **wish** [wɪʃ]   wünschen

Best wishes! [ˈbest wɪʃəs]   Viele Grüße!, Alles Gute!

regards [rɪˈgɑːds]   Grüße

to **attach** [əˈtætʃ]   beifügen, anhängen

Please find attached … [pliːz ˌfaɪnd əˈtætʃt]   Im Anhang sende ich Ihnen …

kind [kaɪnd]   freundlich, nett

Kind/Best regards [kaɪnd/best rɪˈgɑːds]   Freundliche Grüße

in advance [ɪn ədˈvɑːns]   im Voraus

Grammar Practice

53 **birthday party** [ˈbɜːθdeɪ   Geburtstagsparty
      paːti]
   tired [ˈtaɪəd]   müde
   energy [ˈenədʒi]   Energie
   mistake [mɪˈsteɪk]   Fehler
   wonderful [ˈwʌndəfl]   wunderbar
   stressful [ˈstresfl]   anstrengend, stressig
   to wash [wɒʃ]   waschen
   car wash centre [ˈkɑː   Waschanlage
      wɒʃ sentə]
   open [ˈəʊpən]   auf, auf

Consolidation

54 **timeline** [ˈtaɪmlaɪn]   Zeitachse
   school [skuːl]   Schule
   away [əˈweɪ]   weg, fort, entfernt
   another [əˈnʌðə]   noch ein/e/r/s
   film [fɪlm]   Film, Kino
   quickly [ˈkwɪkli]   schnell
   on time [ɒn ˈtaɪm]   pünktlich
   attachment   Anhang
      [əˈtætʃmənt]

Unit 7 - Business Travel

Business Travel

55 **business travel** [ˈbɪznəs   Geschäftsreise
      trævl]
   airport [ˈeəpɔːt]   Flughafen
   bag [bæg]   Tasche, Handtasche
   plane [pleɪn]   Flugzeug
   flight [flaɪt]   Flug
   weather [ˈweðə]   Wetter
   technical [ˈteknɪkl]   technisch
   strike [straɪk]   Streik
   journey [ˈdʒɜːni]   Reise, Fahrt
   agenda [əˈdʒendə]   Tagesordnung
   direction [dəˈrekʃn]   Richtung
   term [tɜːm]   Ausdruck, Begriff
   vocabulary   Vokabular
      [vəˈkæbjələri]

Skills - Travel problems

56 **story** [ˈstɔːri]   Geschichte, Bericht
   facebook [ˈfeɪsbʊk]   Facebook
   search [sɜːtʃ]   Suche, Durchsuchung
   account [əˈkaʊnt]   Konto, Bericht
   pilot [ˈpaɪlət]   Pilot/in
   to wait [weɪt]   warten
   to land [lænd]   landen
   arrival [əˈraɪvl]   Ankunft
   to comment [ˈkɒment]   bemerken, kommentieren
   to fly [flaɪ]   fliegen

without [wɪˈðaʊt]   ohne
waste of time [ˌweɪst əv   Zeitverschwendung
   ˈtaɪm]
waste [weɪst]   Verschwendung, Abfall
disaster [dɪˈzɑːstə]   Katastrophe, Unglück
luggage [ˈlʌgɪdʒ]   Gepäck
hand luggage [ˈhænd   Handgepäck
   lʌgɪdʒ]
enough [ɪˈnʌf]   genug, genügend
finally [ˈfaɪnəli]   schließlich, endlich
to arrive [əˈraɪv]   ankommen, kommen
mean [miːn]   Mittel
transport [ˈtrænspɔːt]   Verkehr, Transport
means of transport   Transportmittel
   [ˌmiːns əv ˈtrænspɔːt]
train [treɪn]   Zug
by car [baɪ ˈkɑː]   mit dem Auto
bus [bʌs]   Bus
to walk [wɔːk]   laufen, spazieren gehen
station [ˈsteɪʃn]   Station, Sender
to drive [draɪv]   fahren
cab [kæb]   Taxi

Skills - Questions about a meeting

57 **to agree** [əˈgriː]   sich einig sein, zustimmen,
                                              vereinbaren
   item [ˈaɪtəm]   Punkt
   tablet [ˈtæblət]   Tafel, Block
   tablet PC [ˌtæblət ˌpiː   Tablet-PC
      ˈsiː]
   participant   Teilnehmer/in
      [pɑːˈtɪsɪpənt]
   quarterly [ˈkwɔːtəli]   vierteljährlich
   result [rɪˈzʌlt]   Ergebnis
   target [ˈtɑːgɪt]   Ziel, Zielscheibe
   to invest [ɪnˈvest]   investieren, anlegen
   investment   Investitionen
      [ɪnˈvestmənt]
   investment decision   Investitionsentscheidung
      [ɪnˈvestmənt dɪsɪʒn]
   to like [laɪk]   gernhaben, mögen, wollen
   decision [dɪˈsɪʒn]   Entscheidung, Entschluss
   million [ˈmɪljən]   Million
   anything [ˈeniθɪŋ]   (irgend)etwas, alles
   frustrating [frʌˈstreɪtɪŋ] frustrierend
   documentation   Unterlagen, Dokumentati-
      [ˌdɒkjəmenˈteɪʃən]   on
   AOB = any other   Verschiedenes, Sonstiges
      business [ˌeɪ əʊ ˈbiː; eni
      ʌðə ˈbɪznəs]
   summary [ˈsʌməri]   Zusammenfassung
   action [ˈækʃn]   Handeln, Aktion

Skills – Giving directions

58	**symbol** [ˈsɪmbl]	Symbol, Zeichen
	to **turn** [tɜːn]	drehen, abbiegen
	to **go past** [gəʊ ˈpɑːst]	vorbeigehen
	straight [streɪt]	gerade
	bank [bæŋk]	Bank
	bookshop [ˈbʊkʃɒp]	Buchhandlung
	pharmacy [ˈfɑːməsi]	Apotheke
	king [kɪŋ]	König
	up King Street [ʌp ˈkɪŋ striːt]	die King Street hoch
	outside [ˌaʊtˈsaɪd]	draußen
	underground [ˈʌndəgraʊnd]	U-Bahn
	underground station [ˈʌndəgraʊnd steɪʃn]	U-Bahn-Station
	bistro [ˈbiːstrəʊ]	Bistro
	far [fɑː]	weit

Skills – In the restaurant

59	**glass** [glɑːs]	Glas
	wine [waɪn]	Wein
	carrot [ˈkærət]	Karotte, Möhre
	ginger [ˈdʒɪndʒə]	Ingwer
	quiche [kiːʃ]	Quiche
	reservation [ˌrezəˈveɪʃn]	Reservierung
	waiter [ˈweɪtə]	Kellner/in, Bedienung
	menu [ˈmenjuː]	Speisekarte, Menü
	today's [təˈdeɪz]	heutig, von heute
	special [ˈspeʃl]	Sonderangebot
	today's special [təˌdeɪz ˈspeʃl]	Tagesgericht, Tageskarte
	board [bɔːd]	Brett, Tafel
	I'd like = I would like [aɪd ˈlaɪk]	Ich hätte gerne
	gin [dʒɪn]	Gin
	tonic [ˈtɒnɪk]	Tonic-Wasser
	I'll be right back. [aɪl bi ˌraɪt ˈbæk]	Ich bin gleich zurück.
	chicken [ˈtʃɪkɪn]	Huhn, Hühnchen
	curry [ˈkʌri]	Currygericht
	mineral water [ˈmɪnərəl wɔːtə]	Mineralwasser
	bottle [ˈbɒtl]	Flasche
	melon [ˈmelən]	Melone
	fish [fɪʃ]	Fisch
	unusual [ʌnˈjuːʒuəl]	ungewöhnlich, außergewöhnlich
	alright [ˌɔːlˈraɪt]	in Ordnung
	how's = how is [haʊz]	wie ist
	to **practise** [ˈpræktɪs]	üben, trainieren, proben
	ready [ˈredi]	bereit, fertig

Grammar

60	to **cost** [kɒst]	kosten
	to **pay** [peɪ]	bezahlen, zahlen
	to **feel** [fiːl]	sich fühlen, empfinden, spüren
	to **fall** [fɔːl]	fallen, stürzen

Grammar Practice

61	**missing** [ˈmɪsɪŋ]	fehlend
	bracket [ˈbrækɪt]	Klammer
	magazine [ˌmægəˈziːn]	Zeitschrift, Illustrierte, Magazin
	price [praɪs]	Preis
	to **translate** [trænsˈleɪt]	übersetzen
	hertz [hɜːts]	Hertz

Consolidation

62	**through** [θruː]	durch, hindurch
	passport [ˈpɑːspɔːt]	Pass, Reisepass
	passport control [ˈpɑːspɔːt kəntrəʊl]	Passkontrolle
	dinner [ˈdɪnə]	Abendessen, Mittagessen
	appointment [əˈpɔɪntmənt]	Termin
	shower [ˈʃaʊə]	Dusche
	alarm [əˈlɑːm]	Wecker, Alarm
	to **phone** [fəʊn]	anrufen
	lucky [ˈlʌki]	glücklich, Glücks-
	starter [ˈstɑːtə]	Vorspeise
	main course [ˈmeɪn kɔːs]	Hauptgericht
	dessert [dɪˈzɜːt]	Nachtisch, Dessert
	food [fuːd]	Essen, Nahrungsmittel
	café [ˈkæfeɪ]	Café
	to **order** [ˈɔːdə]	bestellen
	police [pəˈliːs]	Polizei, Polizisten
	police station [pəˈliːs steɪʃn]	Polizeirevier
	language school [ˈlæŋgwɪdʒ skuːl]	Sprachenschule

A

a, an 7 ein, eine
about 9 über
about 41 circa
account 56 Konto, Bericht
action 57 Handeln, Aktion
active 34 aktiv, tätig
activity 32 Aktivität, Beschäftigung
to **add** 13 hinzufügen
address 26 Adresse, Anschrift
adjective 12 Adjektiv
administration 25 Verwaltung
administrative 8 Verwaltungs…
administrative assistant 8
   Verwaltungsassistent/in
adverb 44 Adverb
after 36 nach, hinter
afternoon 8 Nachmittag
again 42 noch einmal
agenda 55 Tagesordnung
ago 50 vor
to **agree** 57 sich einig sein,
   zustimmen, vereinbaren
air 26 Luft
air conditioning 26 Klimaanlage
airport 55 Flughafen
alarm 62 Wecker, Alarm
all 26 alles, alle
along 25 entlang
along here 25 hier entlang
alphabet 15 Alphabet
alright 59 in Ordnung
also 32 auch, außerdem
always 41 immer
am 7 bin
am 41 morgens, vormittags (lat. ante
   meridiem)
and 7 und
annual 49 Jahres…, jährlich,
   alljährlich
another 54 noch ein/e/r/s
answer 9 Antwort, Lösung
to **answer** 9 antworten, beantworten
to **answer a call** 15 einen Anruf
   entgegennehmen
any 26 (irgend)ein(e/er/s), jede/r/s
   beliebiege
anything 57 (irgend)etwas, alles
AOB = any other business 57
   Verschiedenes, Sonstiges
AOL 44 Firmenname
apostrophe 13 Apostroph
apple 41 Apfel
appointment 62 Termin
April 48 April
are 7 bist, seid, sind
area 17 Gebiet, Gegend, Ort
area code 17 örtliche Vorwahl
around, round 23 um, herum,
   rund um
arrival 56 Ankunft
to **arrive** 56 ankommen, kommen
article 49 Artikel
as 27 wie, so wie, als
asap = as soon as possible 51
   baldmöglichst, so bald wie möglich
to **ask** 9 fragen, bitten, auffordern
assistant 8 Assistent/in
at 7 an, in, bei, auf, um, mit, zu, am,
   für
to **attach** 51 beifügen, anhängen
attachment 54 Anhang
attractive 50 attraktiv, ansprechend
audience 35 Publikum
August 48 August
autumn 48 Herbst
away 54 weg, fort, entfernt

B

back 17 zurück
bad 24 schlecht
bag 55 Tasche, Handtasche
balance 42 Gleichgewicht,
   Ausgeglichenheit
banana 41 Banane
bank 58 Bank
bankrupt 48 bankrott
based 7 einen Sitz haben, wohnen,
   niedergelassen sein
bathroom 25 Badezimmer, Toilette
to **be** 12 sein
to **be active in** 34 aktiv sein,
   vertreten sein
to **be afraid** 20 befürchten
beamer 27 Projektor
because 40 weil, denn
to **become** 35 werden
bed 41 Bett
before 40 bevor, vor
beginning 34 Beginn, Anfang
behind 26 hinter
below 9 unten, unter
Berlin Wall 48 Berliner Mauer
best 9 beste/r/s

Best wishes! 51 Viele Grüße!, Alles
   Gute!
between 25 zwischen
bicycle 46 Fahrrad
big 25 groß
birthday 48 Geburtstag
birthday party 53
   Geburtstagsparty
bistro 58 Bistro
black 25 schwarz
blinds 27 Rollo, Jalousie
blue 8 blau
board 59 Brett, Tafel
book 23 Buch
bookshop 58 Buchhandlung
boss 35 Chef/in, Boss
bottle 59 Flasche
bracket 61 Klammer
brainstorming 7 Brainstorming,
   Ideensammlung
branch 34 Geschäftszweig, Filiale
bread 39 Brot
bread shop 39 Bäckerei
break 40 Pause
breakfast 40 Frühstück
breakfast break 40
   Frühstückspause
briefing 7 Besprechung, Instruktion
brochure 19 Broschüre, Prospekt
brother 48 Bruder
building 30 Gebäude
bus 56 Bus
business 7 Geschäft, Firma
business card 8 Visitenkarte
business contacts 32
   Geschäftskontakte
businessman 29 Geschäftsmann
business travel 55 Geschäftsreise
businesswoman 29 Geschäftsfrau
but 20 aber
to **buy** 32 kaufen
by car 56 mit dem Auto
Bye-bye! 8 Tschüss!

C

cab 56 Taxi
café 62 Café
call 7 Anruf, Gespräch
to **call back** 17 zurückrufen
called 38 namens, mit dem Namen
can 8 können, dürfen
canteen 40 Kantine

capital 17 groß, Haupt-

capital city 42 Hauptstadt, hier:
Firmenname

car 26 Auto, Wagen

card 8 Karte

car park 26 Parkplatz, Parkhaus

carrot 59 Karotte, Möhre

car wash centre 53 Waschanlage

ceiling 27 Decke

cell 32 Zelle, Handy

cell phone 32 Mobiltelefon, Handy

centre (BrE), center (AmE) 26
Anlage, Einrichtung, Center

CEO = Chief Executive Officer 49
Generaldirektor/in,
Geschäftsführer/in,
Vorstandsvorsitzende/r

certainly 19 sicher, natürlich

CFO = Chief Financial Officer 49
Finanzchef/in, Leiter/in der
Finanzabteilung

chair 23 Stuhl

to change 22 ändern, tauschen

change 50 Änderung, Wechsel

to check 9 überprüfen, kontrollieren

chef 35 Küchenchef/in, Koch/
Köchin

chess 43 Schach

chicken 59 Huhn, Hühnchen

chief 47 Chef…

chief financial officer 47 Leiter/in
der Finanzabteilung

child 28 Kind

childcare 26 Kinderbetreuung

childcare centre 26
Kinderbetreuungseinrichtung

to choose 14 wählen, aussuchen

cinema 43 Kino

city 10 Stadt, Großstadt

class 14 Klasse, Kurs

classroom 30 Klassenzimmer

clear 51 klar, offensichtlich

client 37 Kunde/Kundin, Klient/in

clip 45 Clip, Ausschnitt

to close 50 schließen, zumachen

club 41 Klub, Verein

coast 8 Küste

coat 24 Mantel, Jacke

code 17 Vorwahl

coffee 23 Kaffee

coffee break 45 Kaffeepause

coffee machine 23 Kaffeemaschine

colleague 13 Kollege, Kollegin

colour 25 Farbe

to come 19 kommen

to come home 43 nach Hause
kommen

comfortable 29 bequem

to comment 56 bemerken,
kommentieren

communication 49
Kommunikation, Verständigung

company 7 Firma, Gesellschaft

company facts 31 Geschäftszahlen

to compare 45 vergleichen

competition 41 Konkurrenz,
Wettbewerb

to complete 8 beenden, ausfüllen,
vervollständigen

component 32 Teil, Komponente

computer 7 Computer, Rechner

computer game 43 Computerspiel

computer training 7 Computerkurs

concert 43 Konzert

conference 25 Konferenz,
Besprechung

conference room 25
Konferenzraum

to connect 8 verbinden, anschließen

consolidation 14 Festigung

consonant 28 Konsonant

construction 29 Bau, Konstruktion

consultant 49 Berater/in

contact 32 Kontakt

to contact 21 kontaktieren, sich in
Verbindung setzen mit

control 26 Kontrolle

to control 35 beherrschen

control panel 26 Bedienfeld

conversation 11 Gespräch,
Unterhaltung

cool 23 kühl

to coordinate 34 koordinieren,
aufeinander abstimmen

copy 28 Kopie

corner 26 Ecke

Corp. = Corporation 33 Konzern,
Handelsgesellschaft

corporate 49 Unternehmens-,
Firmen-

to correct 13 verbessern, korrigieren

correct 14 richtig, korrekt

to cost 60 kosten

could 51 konnte, dürfte, könnte

country 17 Land, Landschaft

country code 17 Landesvorwahl

course 15 Kurs, Lehrgang

cubic 35 Kubik…, kubisch

cubic metre 35 Kubikmeter

cup 41 Tasse

curry 59 Currygericht

customer 32 Kunde/Kundin

cycling 43 Radfahren

D

date 47 Datum

day 9 Tag

deadline 49 (letzter) Termin

dear 34 lieb, Liebe/r …

December 48 Dezember

to decide 18 entscheiden,
beschließen

decision 57 Entscheidung,
Entschluss

delivery 50 Zustellung, Lieferung

department 8 Abteilung,
Fachbereich

to describe 26 beschreiben

design 8 Entwurf, Design,
Gestaltung

design assistant 16
Designassistent/in

design department 8
Designabteilung

design engineer 16 Konstrukteur/in,
Entwicklungsingenieur/in

designer 8 Designer/in

desk 23 Schreibtisch

dessert 62 Nachtisch, Dessert

detail 51 Einzelheit, Detail

development 9 Entwicklung

dialogue 8 Dialog

different 41 unterschiedlich,
verschieden

difficult 49 schwer, schwierig

dinner 62 Abendessen, Mittagessen

direct 17 direkt, unmittelbar

direction 55 Richtung

direct line 17 Durchwahl

directory 14 Verzeichnis,
Dateiverzeichnis

disaster 56 Katastrophe, Unglück

to discuss 49 besprechen,
diskutieren

discussion 50 Besprechung,
Diskussion

to do 7 tun, machen

document 26 Dokument, Textdatei

documentation 57 Unterlagen, Dokumentation
door 35 Tür
dot 33 Punkt
double 17 doppelt, zwei mal, Doppel-
down 22 hinunter, herunter
to **draw** 30 zeichnen
to **drink** 42 trinken
to **drive** 56 fahren
DVD 37 DVD, digital versatile disc
DVD player 37 DVD-Spieler

E

each 18 jede/r/s, je
early 40 früh, zeitig
eastern 37 östlich, Ost…
to **eat** 39 essen
eating out 43 essen gehen, ins Restaurant gehen
eight 17 acht
eighteen 40 achtzehn
eighteenth 48 achtzehnte/r/s
eighth 48 achte/r/s
eighty 40 achtzig
electrical 37 elektrisch, Elektro…
electrical products 37 Elektrogeräte
electronic 32 elektronisch
electronics 8 Elektronik
electronics company 8 Elektronikhersteller
eleven 40 elf
eleventh 48 elfte/r/s
e-mail, email, mail 8 E-Mail
employee 35 Arbeitnehmer/in, Beschäftigte/r, Angestellte/r
to **end** 28 enden, beenden
end 41 Ende
ending 28 Ende, Endung
energy 53 Energie
engineer 16 Ingenieur/in, Techniker/in
English 7 englisch/e/r
to **enjoy** 43 genießen
enough 56 genug, genügend
entry 41 Eintrag
equipment 23 Ausrüstung
euro 48 Euro
evening 8 Abend
event 7 Veranstaltung

event manager 7 Veranstaltungsmanager
every 39 jede/r/s
everyone 49 jeder, alle
everything 27 alles
ex 42 Ex
except 42 außer, ausgenommen
excerpt 47 Auszug, Ausschnitt
to **exchange** 31 austauschen, tauschen, wechseln
ex-colleague 42 Exkollege/in
to **excuse** 24 entschuldigen
Excuse me. 24 Entschuldigung.
executive 49 geschäftsführend, leitend
exercise 34 Übung
to **exercise** 42 trainieren
to **express** 12 zum Ausdruck bringen, äußern, zeigen
expression 23 Ausdruck
external 49 extern, Außen…
extra 26 Extra…, zusätzlich

F

fabric 35 Stoff, Gewebe
facebook 56 Facebook
facility 26 Anlage
fact 31 Tatsache, Wahrheit
factory 32 Fabrik
fact sheet 34 Datenblatt
fall 48 Herbst
to **fall** 60 fallen, stürzen
false 19 falsch
family 40 Familie
far 58 weit
fashion 45 Trend, Mode
fashion-design company 45 Modedesign-Firma
fashionista 45 Trendsetter/in
Fashion Plus 50 Firmenname
favourite 38 Lieblings…
fax 28 Fax
February 48 Februar
feedback 47 Feedback, Rückmeldung
to **feel** 60 sich fühlen, empfinden, spüren
fifteen 40 fünfzehn
fifteenth 48 fünfzehnte/r/s
fifth 48 fünfte/r/s
fifty 40 fünfzig

figure 50 Zahl
to **fill in** 13 ausfüllen, eintragen
film 54 Film, Kino
finally 56 schließlich, endlich
finance 25 Geld, Finanzwesen
finance department 26 Finanzabteilung
financial 47 Finanz…, finanziell
to **find** 14 finden, feststellen
to **find out** 46 herausfinden
fine 9 gut, in Ordnung
to **finish** 40 fertig sein, beenden, aufhören
first 34 zuerst
first 9 erste/r/s
fish 59 Fisch
five 17 fünf
flight 55 Flug
to **flip** 7 hin- und herspringen
flip chart 7 Flip-Chart
floor 25 Etage, Stockwerk
floor plan 25 Etagenplan
to **fly** 56 fliegen
food 62 Essen, Nahrungsmittel
football 43 Fußball, Football
for 7 für
form 12 Form
to **form** 44 formulieren, bilden
formal 51 förmlich, offiziell, formal
for the first time 47 zum ersten Mal
forty 40 vierzig
four 17 vier
fourteen 40 vierzehn
fourteenth 48 vierzehnte/r/s
fourth 48 vierte/r/s
FP = Fashion Plus 51 Firmenname
free 39 frei, kostenlos
free time 39 Freizeit
frequency 44 Häufigkeit, Frequenz
fresh 41 neu, frisch
Friday 42 Freitag
friend 24 Freund/in, Bekannte/r
friendly 20 freundlich
from 7 von, aus, vor
from … to … 41 von … bis …
front 26 Vorderseite
frustrating 57 frustrierend
full 43 voll, komplett
full-time 43 Vollzeit
further 51 weitere/r/s

G

game 43 Spiel
gap 19 Lücke
garden 30 Garten
gardening 43 Gartenarbeit
general 49 allgemein, Haupt-, General-
genitive 12 Genitiv
to **get** 30 bekommen, werden, kommen
gin 59 Gin
ginger 59 Ingwer
girlfriend 41 Freundin
to **give** 18 geben
glass 59 Glas
global 35 weltweit, global
to **go** 14 gehen
god 48 Gott
good 8 gut
Goodbye! 8 Auf Wiedersehen!, Auf Wiederhören!
Good morning! 8 Guten Morgen!
Google® 46 Firmenname
Gourmet 7 Feinschmecker-Restaurant
grammar 12 Grammatik
grammar practice 13 Grammatikübung
great 26 groß, super
green 25 grün
to **greet** 23 grüßen, begrüßen
grey 25 grau
group 17 Gruppe
gym 43 Fitnesscenter

H

half 40 halb
half past 40 halb (Uhrzeit)
hand luggage 56 Handgepäck
handy 35 nützlich, praktisch
happy 49 glücklich, zufrieden
hard 42 hart
hardware 33 Hardware
hardware department 33 Hardware-Abteilung
to **hate** 44 hassen
to **have** 18 haben
Have a nice day. 18 Einen schönen Tag noch.
to **have breakfast** 40 frühstücken
he 7 er

head 25 Kopf, Leiter/in
headline 47 Schlagzeile, Überschrift
Head of Design 51 Leiter/in der Designabteilung
head office 25 Hauptsitz, Zentrale
Head of Sales 37 Abteilungseiter/in
headquarters 7 Hauptsitz, Zentrale
to **hear** 23 hören, anhören, erfahren
hello 8 hallo
help 18 Hilfe
helpful 51 hilfreich, hilfsbereit
her 7 ihr
here 8 hier, hierher, jetzt
hertz 61 Hertz
Hi! 11 Hallo!
high 26 hoch, groß
to **highlight** 33 unterstreichen
high-speed internet 26 Hochgeschwindigkeits-Internetverbindung
Hightime Electronics 32 Firmenname
him 7 ihn, ihm
hip-hop music 39 Hip-Hop-Musik
his 7 sein
hit 47 Erfolg
hobby 41 Hobby
holiday 16 Urlaub, Ferien
home 39 Zuhause, Wohnung
hot 39 heiß, warm
hotel 49 Hotel
hour 39 Stunde, Zeit
house 41 Haus
how 7 wie
how's = how is 59 wie ist
How are you? 9 Wie geht es dir/Ihnen/euch?
how long 46 wie lange
how many 35 wie viele
how often 39 wie oft
HR = human resources 25 personelle Mittel, Personal
human 25 menschlich
human resources 25 personelle Mittel, Personal
human resources department 26 Personalabteilung
hundred 40 hundert
husband 43 Mann, Ehemann
hyphen 33 Bindestrich, Trennstrich

I

I 7 ich
IBM 48 Firmenname
idea 39 Idee, Plan
to **identify** 48 identifizieren, feststellen
if 51 falls, wenn
important 49 wichtig, einflussreich, bedeutend
in 8 in, bei, herein, da
Inc. 33 eingetragen
to **include** 51 einschließen, einbeziehen
industry 37 Industrie, Branche
informal 12 umgangssprachlich, nicht förmlich
information 8 Informationen, Auskunft
informed 50 informiert
in front of 26 vor
to **introduce oneself** 7 sich vorstellen
to **install** 27 installieren, einbauen
interesting 33 interessant
international 8 international, Auslands…
Internet 7 Internet
into 42 in, hinein
to **introduce** 7 vorstellen
introduction 10 Vorstellung, Einführung
to **invest** 57 investieren, anlegen
investment 57 Investitionen, Anlagekapital
investment decision 57 Investitionsentscheidung
invitation 34 Einladung
ipod 39 iPod
irregular 28 unregelmäßig
is 7 ist
it 7 es
it's about 22 es geht um
item 57 Punkt
IT = Information Technology 14 Informationstechnologie
its 7 sein, ihr

J

January 48 Januar
jeans 45 Jeans
job 7 Stelle, Arbeitsplatz, Arbeit
job title 7 Berufsbezeichnung, Stellenbezeichnung
to **jog** 42 joggen
to **join** 50 sich anschließen
journey 55 Reise, Fahrt
July 47 Juli
June 47 Juni
just 8 nur, wenig, etwas
Just a moment. 8 Einen Moment, bitte.

K

to **keep** 41 halten, bewahren
to **keep in touch** 41 in Verbindung bleiben
key 7 Schlüssel…
Key Language 7 wichtige Redewendungen, Schlüsselwörter
kind 51 freundlich, nett
Kind/Best regards 51 Freundliche Grüße
king 58 König
to **know** 7 wissen, kennen

L

to **land** 56 landen
language 7 Sprache
language school 62 Sprachenschule
laptop 7 Laptop
large 35 groß
last 40 letzte/r/s
last time 40 letztes Mal
late 41 spät
later 19 später
launch 48 Einführung, Präsentation
leader 10 Leiter/in, Vorsitzende/r
to **learn** 7 lernen
to **leave** 19 verlassen, hinterlassen
to **leave a message** 19 eine Nachricht hinterlassen
left 25 links, nach links
lesson 41 Unterricht, Lektion
to **let** 34 lassen
letter 51 Buchstabe
life 42 Leben
lifeline 41 hier: Verbindung
lift 29 Fahrstuhl, Aufzug
like 20 wie

to **like** 57 gernhaben, mögen, wollen
line 17 Leitung, Telefonanschluss, Linie
list 7 Liste
to **listen** 8 hören, zuhören
to **live** 36 leben, wohnen
local 41 örtlich
location 26 Lage, Ort, Platz
logistics 10 Logisitk, Versorgung
long 42 lang, weit, lange
to **look** 7 ansehen, schauen
to **look at** 7 ansehen, betrachten
lot 26 Menge, Gelände
loudspeaker 27 Lautsprecher
to **love** 39 lieben
Ltd = Limited 33 GmbH
lucky 62 glücklich, Glücks-
luggage 56 Gepäck
lunch 28 Mittagessen
lunch break 42 Mittagspause
lunch hour 39 Mittagspause
lunchtime 41 Mittagszeit

M

machine 23 Maschine
magazine 61 Zeitschrift, Illustrierte, Magazin
to **mail, e-mail, email** 7 (per Post) schicken, mailen
main 34 Haupt…
main course 62 Hauptgericht
major 37 groß, bedeutend
to **make** 32 machen, herstellen
to **make photocopies** 41 fotokopieren
making 18 Herstellung
man 18 Mann, Mensch
to **manage** 43 leiten, führen, managen
management 51 Führung, Management
manager 7 Geschäftsführer/in, Manager/in, Leiter/in
to **manage the house** 43 den Haushalt machen
to **manufacture** 32 herstellen, produzieren, fertigen
many 35 viele
map 31 Plan, Karte
March 48 März
marker 7 Textmarker, Filzstift
market 35 Markt

marketing 7 Marketing, Vermarktung
marketing meeting 7 Marketingbesprechung
to **match** 7 zuordnen
May 47 Mai
me 17 ich, mich, mir
meal 41 Mahlzeit, Essen
mean 56 Mittel
means of transport 56 Transportmittel
to **meet** 7 (sich) treffen
meeting 7 Besprechung, Sitzung, Treffen
melon 59 Melone
member 14 Mitglied
memory 49 Gedächtnis, Erinnerung
memory card 49 Speicherkarte
to **mention** 25 erwähnen
menu 59 Speisekarte, Menü
message 15 Nachricht
method 48 Methode
metre 35 Meter
microphone 27 Mikrofon
mid 47 Mitte
midday 41 Mittag
middle 27 Mitte
mid-summer 47 Mittsommer, Hochsommer
million 57 Million
mineral water 59 Mineralwasser
mini 27 sehr klein
minute 42 Minute, Moment
missing 61 fehlend
mistake 53 Fehler
mobile 21 Handy, Mobiltelefon
mobile phone 32 Mobiltelefon, Handy
module 34 Modul, Baustein
moment 8 Moment, Augenblick
Monday 42 Montag
monitor 23 Monitor, Bildschirm
month 46 Monat
more 33 mehr
morning 8 Morgen, Vormittag
most 28 der/die/das meiste, die meisten
motivation 49 Motivation
mouse 23 Maus
to **move** 50 (sich) bewegen, umziehen
movie 42 Film
MP3 player 37 MP3-Spieler

Mr 14 Herr
Mrs 17 Frau
Ms 14 Frau
much 33 viel
music 39 Musik
music producer 43
   Musikproduzent/in
must 41 müssen
my 7 mein
myself 34 mich

N
to **name** 7 nennen
name 7 Name
nationality 31 Staatsangehörigkeit,
   Nationalität
need 25 brauchen, nötig haben,
   erfordern
negative 12 Verneinung, Negation
negative 12 negativ, verneinend,
   verneint
nervous 49 nervös, aufgeregt
network 8 Netzwerk
networking site 8 soziales
   Netzwerk im Internet
neutral 51 neutral, unbeteiligt
never 39 nie, niemals
new 8 neu
news 41 Nachricht/en
newsletter 39 Rundschreiben,
   Newsletter
newspaper 39 Zeitung
next to 25 neben
nice 18 schön, nett, gut
night 45 Nacht, Abend
nine 17 neun
nineteen 40 neunzehn
nineteenth 48 neunzehnte/r/s
ninety 40 neunzig
ninth 48 neunte/r/s
no 12 nein
No problem. 20 Kein Problem.
normal 41 normal, üblich
normally 44 normalerweise,
   gewöhnlich
north 35 Norden
not 7 nicht
Not bad. 24 Nicht schlecht.
note 13 Notiz, Nachricht,
   Anmerkung
noun 28 Substantiv, Nomen
November 48 November

now 7 jetzt, sofort, nun
number 15 Zahl, Nummer, Anzahl

O
o'clock 41 Uhr
object 20 Gegenstand, Objekt
objective 7 Ziel
object pronoun 20
   Objektpronomen
October 48 Oktober
of 13 von, aus
of course 17 natürlich,
   selbstverständlich
offer 34 Angebot
to **offer** 46 anbieten
office 8 Büro, Arbeitszimmer
office equipment 23 Büromaterial,
   Büroausstattung, Büroeinrichtung
officer 47 Beamter/Beamtin
office skills 8 Fähigkeiten/
   Fertigkeiten für die Büroarbeit
office worker 8 Büroangestellte/r
often 37 oft, häufig
OK 17 O.K., in Ordnung
old 48 alt, ehemalig
on 8 auf, an
once 42 einmal, einst, früher einmal
once a week 42 einmal in der
   Woche
one 17 eins, ein/e
online 41 online, Online…
only 41 einzige/r/s
on Monday(s) 42 Montag, montags
on the left 25 links, auf der linken
   Seite
on the right 25 rechts, auf der
   rechten Seite
on time 54 pünktlich
to **open** 47 aufmachen, öffnen
open 53 auf, auf
to **operate** 34 arbeiten, in Betrieb
   sein
operation 34 Betrieb
opposite 25 gegenüber
or 12 oder
orange 25 orange
order 18 Reihenfolge, Auftrag,
   Bestellung
to **order** 62 bestellen
order number 22 Bestellnummer,
   Auftragsnummer
ordinal 47 Ordinal-, Ordnungs-

to **organize** 34 organisieren
other 7 andere/r/s
our 7 unser
out 15 hinaus, heraus, nicht da,
   nicht zu Hause
out of the office 15 nicht im Büro
outside 58 draußen
over 25 über
over here 25 hier drüben
overtime 40 Überstunden

P
page 16 Seite, Webseite
panel 26 Kontrolltafel, Schalttafel
paper 26 Papier
PA = Personal Assistant 51
   persönliche/r Assistent/in
park 26 Park
to **park** 26 parken
parking lot 26 Parkplatz
part 8 Teil
participant 57 Teilnehmer/in
partner 8 Partner/in
part-time 43 halbtags
party 47 Party
passport 62 Pass, Reisepass
passport control 62 Passkontrolle
past 40 nach
past 47 Vergangenheit
pasta 39 Nudeln
to **pay** 60 bezahlen, zahlen
pen 30 Stift
people 7 Leute, Menschen
perfect 27 perfekt, fehlerfrei
performance 47 Leistung
performance review 47
   Leistungsüberblick
person 24 Mensch, Person
personal pronoun 12
   Personalpronomen
pharmacy 58 Apotheke
phone 8 Telefon
to **phone** 62 anrufen
phone number 17 Telefonnummer
photo 7 Foto
photocopier, copier 23
   Fotokopierer
photocopy 41 Fotokopie
phrase 14 Satz
picture 15 Bild
pilot 56 Pilot/in
pink 25 rosa

place 15 Ort, Stelle, Platz
plan 25 Plan
to plan 34 planen, vorhaben
plane 55 Flugzeug
plant 23 Pflanze
to play 43 spielen
plc = public limited company 33
  an der Börse notierte
  Aktiengesellschaft
to please 24 zufriedenstellen
please 8 bitte
plural 23 Plural, Mehrzahl
pm 40 nachmittags, abends (lat.
  post meridiem)
pointer 27 Zeiger
police 62 Polizei, Polizisten
police station 62 Polizeirevier
policy 47 Politik, Grundsatz
portable 37 tragbar
portfolio 50 Mappe
position 45 Position, Lage,
  Standpunkt
positive 12 positiv, bejahend
possession 12 Besitz
possessive adjective 12
  besitzanzeigendes Fürwort
possessive determiner 12
  besitzanzeigender Begleiter
possible 49 möglich
post 41 Post
power point 26 Power Point™,
  Steckdose
practice 13 Übung
to practise 59 üben, trainieren,
  proben
to prefer 43 vorziehen, etwas lieber
  tun
presentation 27 Präsentation,
  Vortrag
price 61 Preis
printer 26 Drucker
problem 20 Problem, Aufgabe
to produce 32 herstellen,
  produzieren
producer 43 Hersteller/in,
  Produzent/in
product 34 Produkt
production 9 Herstellung,
  Produktion
production area 25
  Produktionsbereich,
  Herstellungsbereich

production manager 10
  Produktionsleiter/in
production worker 37
  Produktionsarbeiter/in
product line 50 Produktlinie
profile 8 Profil, Beschreibung
project 7 Projekt, Vorhaben, Arbeit
project assistant 16
  Projektassistent/in
project leader 10 Projektleiter/in
project manager 8 Projektleiter/in,
  Auftragsleiter/in
projector 26 Projektor
project specialist 10
  Projektspezialist/in, Experte/
  Expertin
project update 7
  Projektaktualisierung
pronoun 12 Pronomen, Fürwort
PR = public relations 34
  Öffentlichkeitsarbeit, Werbung
public 16 öffentlich, Staats…
public holiday 16 Feiertag
purchasing 25 Einkauf
purchasing department 30
  Abteilung Einkauf
purple 25 lila
to put 18 legen, setzen, stellen
to put in order 18 in eine
  Reihenfolge bringen

Q

quarter 40 Viertel
quarterly 57 vierteljährlich
question 9 Frage
question word 12 Fragewort
quiche 59 Quiche
quickly 54 schnell
quite 41 ziemlich, völlig

R

radio 39 Radio
rarely 44 selten
reaction 9 Reaktion
to read 7 lesen
ready 59 bereit, fertig
real 14 echt
really 33 wirklich, sehr
to receive 35 erhalten, bekommen
reception 25 Rezeption, Empfang
reception area 26 Empfangsbereich
receptionist 9 Empfangschef/in

red 25 rot
regards 51 Grüße
regular 47 regelmäßig, normal
regularly 39 regelmäßig, oft
to remember 15 sich erinnern an
to repeat 17 wiederholen
reply 51 Antwort
to report 46 berichten
report 47 Bericht
request 20 Bitte
research 9 Forschung
research and development
  department 13 Forschungs- und
  Entwicklungsabteilung
reservation 59 Reservierung
resources 25 Mittel, Ressourcen
response 20 Antwort, Reaktion
rest 25 Ruhe, Pause
restaurant 26 Restaurant
restroom 25 Toilette
to restructure 49 umstrukturieren
result 57 Ergebnis
review 47 Überprüfung, Rezension
revision 15 Korrektur,
  Überarbeitung, Änderung
right 9 richtig, rechts
road 33 Straße
role 22 Rolle
room 25 Raum
round 25 (rund)herum
routine 36 Routine, Gewohnheit
routine activity 36 Routine-
  handlung

S

salad 39 Salat
sale 25 Verkauf
sales administration center 47
  Abteilung für Auftragsabwicklung
sales department 26
  Verkaufsabteilung
sales figure 50 Verkaufszahl
sales manager 29 Verkaufsleiter/in
sales representative 33 Vertreter/in
same 45 der/die/das gleiche
sandwich 39 Sandwich
Saturday 42 Samstag
to say 17 sagen, sprechen
schedule 39 Zeitplan
school 54 Schule
search 56 Suche, Durchsuchung
second 48 zweite/r/s

sector **22** Bereich

to **see** **23** sehen, verstehen, besuchen

to **sell** **32** verkaufen

seminar **29** Seminar

to **send** **7** schicken, verschicken, abschicken

senior **51** ranghöher, dienstälter

sentence **8** Satz

sentence part **8** Satzteil

September **47** September

service **49** Dienst

seven **17** sieben

seventeen **40** siebzehn

seventeenth **48** siebzehnte/r/s

seventh **48** siebte/r/s

seventy **40** siebzig

shareholder **49** Aktionär/in

she **7** sie

sheet **34** Blatt

shop **26** Laden, Geschäft

shopping **43** Einkaufen, Einkäufe

short **12** kurz, klein

short form **12** Kurzform

to **show** **25** zeigen, vorzeigen

shower **62** Dusche

to **show round** **25** herumführen

sick **16** krank, übel

side **27** Seite

simple present **36** einfache Form der Gegenwart, Präsens

singular **28** Singular, Einzahl

site **8** Internetseite

six **17** sechs

sixteen **40** sechzehn

sixteenth **48** sechzehnte/r/s

sixth **48** sechste/r/s

sixty **40** sechzig

sketch **31** Skizze

sketch map **31** gezeichnete Karte

skill **8** Geschick, Fähigkeit, Fertigkeit

to **sleep** **41** schlafen

small **11** klein

small talk **11** Small Talk, Konversation

smartphone **41** Smartphone

so **9** also

software **8** Software

software designer **8** Software-Entwickler/in

some **35** etwas, einige, ungefähr

something **49** etwas

sometimes **39** manchmal

soon **51** bald

Sorry. **8** Tut mir leid., Entschuldigung.

to **sort** **41** sortieren

to **sound** **12** klingen, sich anhören

soup **39** Suppe

south **35** Süden

to **speak** **9** sprechen, reden

to **speak Russian** **20** Russisch sprechen

special **34** Sonder-, speziell

special **59** Sonderangebot

specialist **10** Spezialist/in, Fachmann/frau

to **specialize** **33** sich spezialisieren

speed **26** Geschwindigkeit

to **spell** **19** buchstabieren, orthografisch richtig schreiben

spelling **17** Rechtschreibung, Schreibweise

spoken language **12** gesprochene Sprache

sport **26** Sport, Sportart

sports club **41** Sportverein

sports facilities **26** Sportanlagen, Sportplatz

sporty **43** sportlich

spring **48** Frühling

squash **43** Squash

staff **26** Personal

to **start** **36** anfangen, beginnen

starter **62** Vorspeise

statement **13** Aussage, Erklärung

station **56** Station, Sender

to **stay** **41** bleiben, wohnen

to **stay in touch** **41** in Verbindung bleiben

still **48** immer noch

to **stop** **50** anhalten, aufhören, beenden

story **56** Geschichte, Bericht

straight **58** gerade

strategy **50** Strategie

street **8** Straße

stress **45** Stress, Belastung

stressful **53** anstrengend, stressig

strike **55** Streik

structure **51** Struktur, Aufbau

student **43** Student/in, Kursteilnehmer/in

stylish **50** modisch, stilvoll

subject **20** Thema, Subjekt

subject pronoun **20** Subjektpronomen

success **50** Erfolg

successful **51** erfolgreich

summary **57** Zusammenfassung

summer **47** Sommer

Sunday **42** Sonntag

sunny **30** sonnig

supermarket **41** Supermarkt

supplier **32** Lieferant/in

to **supply** **32** liefern

sure **20** sicher

to **switch off** **40** ausschalten

to **switch on** **40** anschalten

symbol **58** Symbol, Zeichen

system **49** System

T

table **26** Tisch

tablet **57** Tafel, Tablette, Block

tablet PC **57** Tablet-PC

to **take** **15** nehmen

to **take a message** **15** eine Nachricht entgegennehmen

talk **11** Gespräch, Gerede

to **talk** **39** reden, sprechen, sich unterhalten

target **57** Ziel, Zielscheibe

task **17** Aufgabe

taxi **46** Taxi

taxi bicycle **46** Fahrradtaxi

tea **41** Tee

team **7** Mannschaft, Team

technical **55** technisch

technology **14** Technologie

telephone **7** Telefon

telephone call, phone call **7** Telefonanruf

telephone phrase **14** Redewendung für Gespräche am Telefon

to **tell** **14** erzählen, sagen

ten **27** zehn

tennis **43** Tennis

tenth **48** zehnte/r/s

term **55** Ausdruck, Begriff

text **7** Text, SMS

tgif = Thank God It's Friday! **48** Zum Glück ist bald Wochenende!

thanks **9** danke (umgangssprachlich)

Thank you. **8** Danke.

Thank you for calling. **18** Danke für den Anruf.

Thank you for your call. 18 Danke für deinen/Ihren/euren Anruf.

Thank you for your help. 18 Vielen Dank für deine/Ihre/eure Hilfe.

that 9 das, der/die/das

that's all 26 das ist alles

That's right. 9 Das stimmt.

the 7 der, die, das, die (Plural)

theatre 43 Theater

their 7 ihr

them 20 sie, ihnen

then 9 dann

there 22 da, dort, dahin, dorthin

there's 26 es gibt, da ist

these 13 diese, die (hier)

they 7 sie, man

thing 7 Ding, Sache

to think 26 denken, glauben

third 48 dritte/r/s

thirteen 40 dreizehn

thirteenth 48 dreizehnte/r/s

thirtieth 48 dreißigste/r/s

thirty 40 dreißig

this 8 dies, das, diese/r/s hier

This way, please. 25 Hier entlang bitte.

those 49 diese

thousand 48 tausend

three 16 drei

three times a day 42 dreimal am Tag

through 62 durch, hindurch

Thursday 42 Donnerstag

to tick 19 abhaken, ankreuzen

time 39 Zeit, Mal

timeline 54 Zeitachse

tired 53 müde

title 7 Titel

to 7 in, mit, zu

today 9 heute, heutzutage

today's 59 heutig, von heute

today's special 59 Tagesgericht, Tageskarte

to-do list 7 Aufgabenliste

together 40 zusammen

toilet 25 Toilette

tomorrow 48 morgen

tonic 59 Tonic-Wasser

too 18 zu, auch

top 49 Spitzen…

touch 41 Verbindung

tour 25 Tour, Rundgang

town 19 Stadt

train 56 Zug

training 7 Ausbildung

training course 15 Übungskurs

to translate 61 übersetzen

transport 56 Verkehr, Transport

to travel 37 reisen, fahren

trip 16 Reise, Fahrt

true 19 wahr, richtig

Tuesday 42 Dienstag

to turn 58 drehen, abbiegen

TV 41 Fernsehen, Fernseher

twelfth 48 zwölfte/r/s

twelve 40 zwölf

twentieth 48 zwanzigste/r/s

twenty 40 zwanzig

twice 42 zwei Mal

two 13 zwei

type 33 Art, Sorte

U

under 26 unter

underground 58 U-Bahn

underground station 58 U-Bahn-Station

to underline 7 unterstreichen

underscore 33 Unterstrich

to understand 7 verstehen

unfriendly 12 unfreundlich

unhappy 49 unglücklich, unzufrieden

unit 7 Einheit, Abteilung

until 41 bis

unusual 59 ungewöhnlich, außergewöhnlich

update 7 Aktualisierung, Update

to update 41 auf den neuesten Stand bringen, aktualisieren

up King Street 58 die King Street hoch

us 20 uns, wir

to use 8 benutzen, verwenden, gebrauchen

usually 39 normalerweise, gewöhnlich

V

verb 12 Verb

very 26 sehr

very much 33 sehr

Very nice. 26 Sehr schön., Sehr gut.

video 27 Video

video clip 45 Videoclip

video conference 27 Videokonferenz

video conference facilities 29 technische Anlage für eine Videokonferenz

to visit 50 besuchen, besichtigen

visit 50 Besuch, Besichtigung

visitor 23 Besucher/in

vocabulary 55 Vokabular

W

to wait 56 warten

waiter 59 Kellner/in, Bedienung

walk 43 Spaziergang, Wanderung

to walk 56 laufen, spazieren gehen

wall 26 Wand, Mauer

to want 41 wollen, mögen, brauchen

warehouse 25 Lager, Lagerhalle

to wash 53 waschen

waste 56 Verschwendung, Abfall

waste of time 56 Zeitverschwendung

to watch 39 schauen, zuschauen

to watch TV 41 fernsehen

water 23 Wasser

water cooler 23 Trinkwasserkühler

way 25 Weg, Richtung

WC 25 WC, Toilette

we 7 wir

weather 55 Wetter

web 30 (World Wide) Web

web address 30 Web-Adresse

website 7 Website

website text 7 Website-Text

Wednesday 42 Mittwoch

week 39 Woche

weekend 42 Wochenende

welcome 7 willkommen

well 25 also, nun, gut

what 7 was , welche/r, was für ein

What's your name? 7 Wie heißen Sie?, Wie heißt du?

What's your phone number? 17 Wie lautet deine/Ihre Telefonnummer?

what about … 42 was ist mit …

What time is it? 41 Wie spät ist es?

when 36 wann, wenn

where 7 wo

Abarth [əˈbɑːt]; **38**

Aberdeen [ˌæbəˈdiːn]; **32**

America [əˈmerɪkə]; **35**

American [əˈmerɪkən]; **37**

Amsterdam [ˈæmstədæm]; **34**

Asia [ˈeɪʃə]; **49**

Asian [ˈeɪʃn]; **49**

Australia [ɒˈstreɪliə]; **31**

Australian [ɒˈstreɪliən]; **31**

Austria [ˈɒstriə]; **14**

Austrian [ˈɒstriən]; **38**

Barbados [bɑːˈbeɪdɒs]; **41**

Beijing [beɪˈdʒɪŋ]; **13**

Berlin [bɜːˈlɪn]; **10**

Birmingham [ˈbɜːmɪŋəm]; **53**

Blue Coast Electronics [bluː kəʊst ɪˌlekˈtrɒnɪks]; **8**

Bologna [bəˈlanjə]; **38**

Brazil [brəˈzɪl]; **31**

Brighton [ˈbraɪtən]; **49**

British [ˈbrɪtɪʃ]; **31**

Buenos Aires [bʊenəs ˈaɪrəs]; **35**

CA = California [siː eɪ; ˌkælɪˈfɔːniə]; **8**

Canada [ˈkænədə]; **31**

Canadian [kəˈneɪdiən]; **32**

Chicago [ʃɪˈkɑːgəʊ]; **36**

China [ˈtʃaɪnə]; **31**

Chinatown [ˈtʃaɪnətaʊn]; **62**

Chinese [ˌtʃaɪˈniːz]; **21**

Danish [ˈdeɪnɪʃ]; **31**

Denmark [ˈdenmɑːk]; **31**

Dubai [ˈdubaɪ]; **29**

Dundee [dʌnˈdiː]; **37**

Dutch [dʌtʃ]; **31**

England [ˈɪŋglənd]; **25**

Europe [ˈjʊərəp]; **32**

European [ˌjʊərəˈpiːən]; **32**

Finland [ˈfɪnlənd]; **31**

Florida [ˈflɒrɪdə]; **11**

France [frɑːns]; **31**

French [frentʃ]; **31**

German [ˈdʒɜːmən]; **19**

Germany [ˈdʒɜːməni]; **9**

Great Britain [ˌgreɪt ˈbrɪtn]; **49**

Heathrow [ˈhiːθrəʊ]; **56**

India [ˈɪndiə]; **31**

Ireland [ˈaɪələnd]; **18**

Italian [ɪˈtæliən]; **38**

Italy [ˈɪtəli]; **31**

Jakarta [dʒəˈkɑːtə]; **35**

Japan [dʒəˈpæn]; **31**

JFK [ˌdʒeɪ ef ˈkeɪ]; **62**

Lehman Brothers [ˈliːmən brʌðəz]; **48**

Liverpool [ˈlɪvəpuːl]; **56**

London [ˈlʌndən]; **28**

Manhattan [ˌmænˈhætn]; **62**

Mexico [ˈmeksɪkəʊ]; **45**

Monterrey [mɒntəˈreɪ]; **57**

Montreal [ˌmɒntriˈɔːl]; **32**

Munich [ˈmjuːnɪk]; **8**

Netherlands [ˈneðələndz]; **31**

New York [ˌnjuː ˈjɔːk]; **11**

North America [ˌnɔːθ əˈmerɪkə]; **35**

Oakland [ˈəʊklænd]; **49**

Poland [ˈpəʊlənd]; **34**

Polish [ˈpəʊlɪʃ]; **34**

Portugal [ˈpɔːtʃəgəl]; **31**

Poznań [ˈpɒznæn]; **34**

Prague [prɑːg]; **59**

Profone [prəʊˈfəʊn]; **38**

Romania [ruˈmeɪniə]; **37**

Rome [rəʊm]; **55**

Russia [ˈrʌʃə]; **35**

Russian [ˈrʌʃn]; **20**

San Diego [sæn ˈdiegəʊ]; **22**

San Francisco [sæn frænˈsɪskəʊ]; **8**

Scotland [ˈskɒtlənd]; **32**

Shanghai [ʃæŋˈhaɪ]; **13**

South America [ˌsaʊθ əˈmerɪkə]; **35**

Southampton [saʊθˈhæmptn]; **50**

Spain [speɪn]; **31**

Spanish [ˈspænɪʃ]; **21**

Stansted [ˈstænstəd]; **56**

Stirling [ˈstɜːlɪŋ]; **37**

Sweden [ˈswiːdn]; **31**

Swiss [swɪs]; **31**

Switzerland [ˈswɪtsələnd]; **33**

Syria [ˈsɪriə]; **59**

Texas [ˈteksəs]; **13**

Turkey [ˈtɜːki]; **35**

UK=United Kingdom [juː ˈkeɪ; juˌnaɪtɪd ˈkɪŋdəm]; **29**

USA = United States of America [juːesˈeɪ; juˌnaɪtɪd ˌsteɪts əv əˈmerɪkə]; **8**

Vancouver [ˈvæŋkuːvə]; **37**

Venezuela [ˌvenəˈzweɪlə]; **45**

Vienna [vɪˈenə]; **14**

Zurich [ˈzʊərɪk]; **33**

Copyright

Fotos

1	Copyright		00:47
Unit 1			
2	p. 8	ex. 1	00:37
3	p. 8	ex. 3	01:04
4	p. 9	ex. 4	00:43
5	p. 9	ex. 5	00:58
6	p. 10	ex. 1	00:38
7	p. 10	ex. 2	00:39
8	p. 11	ex. 4	00:42
9	p. 14	ex. 4	01:04
Unit 2			
10	p. 15	ex. 3	00:49
11	p. 16	ex. 1	00:54
12	p. 16	ex. 3	01:39
13	p. 17	ex. 1	01:07
14	p. 17	ex. 2	00:46
15	p. 17	ex. 3	01:39
16	p. 17	ex. 5	01:24
17	p. 18	ex. 1	01:49
18	p. 18	ex. 2	01:16
19	p. 19	ex. 4+5	02:19
20	p. 19	ex. 6	02:01
21	p. 22	ex. 2	01:11

22	p. 22	ex. 3	01:13
23	p. 22	ex. 4	01:22
Unit 3			
24	p. 23	ex. 2	01:09
25	p. 24	ex. 1	00:32
26	p. 24	ex. 3	00:36
27	p. 25	ex. 1	00:37
28	p. 25	ex. 2	00:49
29	p. 25	ex. 2	00:40
30	p. 25	ex. 4	01:28
31	p. 26	ex. 1	01:29
32	p. 26,	ex. 3	00:57
33	p. 27	ex. 6	01:14
Unit 4			
34	p. 30	ex. 4	01:56
35	p. 32	ex. 1	01:09
36	p. 32	ex. 2	01:17
37	p. 33	ex. 1	01:26
38	p. 33	ex. 3	02:36
39	p. 35	ex. 5	01:14
40	p. 35	ex. 6	01:14
41	p. 38	ex. 2	02:42

Unit 5			
42	p. 39	ex. 3	01:12
43	p. 40	ex. 2	01:44
44	p. 40	ex. 3	01:24
45	p. 40	ex. 4	01:11
46	p. 42	ex. 1+2	01:40
47	p. 43	ex. 1	00:51
48	p. 45	ex. 3	01:11
Unit 6			
49	p. 48	ex. 2	01:04
50	p. 48	ex. 3	00:44
51	p. 48	ex. 4	01:17
52	p. 50	ex. 1	01:50
53	p. 54	ex. 3	01:10
Unit 7			
54	p. 55	ex. 1	00:54
55	p. 55	ex. 2	00:56
56	p. 56	ex. 1	01:52
57	p. 57	ex. 3	01:52
58	p. 58	ex. 3	01:40
59	p. 59	ex. 1	01:24
60	p. 59	ex. 3	00:55
Total running time			**72:00**

Studio:
Clarity Studio Berlin

Aufnahmeleitung:
Christian Schmitz

Tontechnik:
Pascal Thinius

Regie:
Christine House
Rani Kumar
Christian Schmitz

Sprecher/innen:
Shaunessy Ashdown
Laura Cameron
Tania Carlin
Steve Ellery
Marianne Graffam
Manon Kahle
Martin Klemrath
Kevin McAleer
Helena Prince
Ian H. Smith
Darren Smith
Brittani Sonnenberg
Ian Wood
Felix Würgler